SACRED
Sexuality

*Throughout the ages creativity has been one of the ways
in which people have expressed their religious beliefs.
The aim of* The Sacred Arts *is to explore those arts
which reflect the spiritual vision of humanity and
contain truth as well as beauty.*

*The divine truth is expressed in many forms – from
architecture to music, from dance to landscape.*

*The discovery of deeper meaning within outer forms
brings us closer to our centre and to the sacred traditions
which are so undervalued in our modern world.*

IN THE SAME SERIES:

Sacred Architecture *by AT Mann*

SACRED
Sexuality

A T MANN
AND
JANE LYLE

ELEMENT

Shaftesbury, Dorset • Rockport, Massachusetts • Brisbane, Queensland

First published in Great Britain in 1995 by

ELEMENT BOOKS LIMITED

Shaftesbury, Dorset SP7 8BP

Published in the USA in 1995 by

ELEMENT BOOKS, INC.

PO Box 830, Rockport, MA 01966

Published in Australia in 1995 by

ELEMENT BOOKS LIMITED

for JACARANDA WILEY LIMITED

33 Park Road, Milton, Brisbane 4064

THE BRIDGEWATER BOOK COMPANY

Design by *Sarah Stanley*

Picture Research by *Felicity Cox*

Page make-up by *Jane and Chris Lanaway*

Repro by *Appletone Graphics*

Printed and bound in Great Britain by BPC Paulton Books Ltd

British Library Cataloguing in Publication

Data available

Library of Congress Cataloging in Publication

Data available

ISBN 1-85230-658-0

ACKNOWLEDGEMENTS

To my wife Lise-Lotte

I would like to thank my wife Lise-Lotte Mann for
her interest in this book and for her invaluable feed-
back about the ideas expressed here. Thanks also to
Erik and Tove Ansvang, Paul Birkholm, Rufus
Camphausen, Apollonia, and Henning Argyll Olsen
for their inspiration and book loans, and to John
Baldock and Linda Quayle of Element for their help.

A T MANN

For Aphrodite Pandemos

Heartfelt thanks to Susy Kennard for her invaluable
help with the intricacies of Courtly Love, and
Geraldine Leale for her outstanding alchemical advice
and support.

JANE LYLE

ABOUT THE AUTHORS

A T Mann is an American architect, graphic
designer, astrologer and counsellor. He lives in
Denmark, and is the author of a number of books
including *The Elements of the Tarot, Sacred Architecture,
Life Time Astrology, The Divine Plot* and *Millennium
Prophecies*.

Jane Lyle has studied astrology and tarot symbolism
for more than ten years and has lived in Canada,
Greece and the United States. Her previous books,
which include *Body Language, Lovers' Tarot* and
Women's Wisdom, have been translated into several
languages. She has also written for a variety of
national newspapers and women's magazines.

CONTENTS

Introduction

IN THE SELF-SAME POINT WHERE THE SOUL IS MADE SENSUAL, IN THE SELF-SAME POINT IS THE CITY OF GOD ORDAINED FROM WITHOUT BEGINNING.

Juliana of Norwich (1343–1415)

Sacred sexuality belongs to our ancient past, and to our future. It unites mind, body and spirit. In a world divorced from instinct, it offers a vibrant, visceral and regenerative way forward. This concept, and its teachings, acknowledges and venerates the life-force which animates all living things. And yet it is nothing new, as we intend to demonstrate. Sacred sexuality has been particularly repressed in Western society, and so we have explored its European history in some detail. However, the links between natural, sensual pleasures and religious feelings are universal and profoundly innocent.

Placing the words 'sacred' and 'sexuality' together creates an uncomfortable paradox for many people. How can sexuality, with its host of negative connotations, be part of the spiritual realms? This reaction serves as a reflection of our present-day confusion. In our modern world sexuality is largely condemned by major religions. We are taught that it is dark, degenerate, a primary sin of humanity, to be countered only by suppression and redeemed by celibacy. Moralists and religious fundamentalists of all persuasions consider it an evil influence, capable of destroying faith, and tempting good souls to sin, hell and torment. Christian dogma says that sexuality is the cause of 'the fall' of human-

ity, symbolized by the seductive serpent in the Garden of Eden. Sex is symbolic of hell, as purity is of heaven. We believe these views are archaic and destructive.

The compelling nature of sexual desire has made it a prime target for commercial exploitation. For centuries the sex industry has been equated with pornography and prostitution which, by extension, have become seen as devices which suppress female sexuality, diminish male sexuality, and contribute towards an atmosphere of violence and mistrust. Gender warfare is endemic in our society, while political correctness serves to further inhibit and restrict fluid self-expression. Feminists wage philosophical battle with masculinists, and vice versa. Sexuality is increasingly equated with aggressors and victims, locked in an endless conflict which neither can win, or relinquish.

Sigmund Freud, who pioneered modern psychoanalysis, considered sexuality to be at the root of most psychological disorders. He suggested that these originate with the frustrations and repressions associated with our first contacts with our parents – with mother during and after birth, and with father in earliest infancy. In his view, sexuality is inevitably distorted, causing both individual violence and the universal human tendency towards violence. But even psychological concepts of sexuality are quite fixed and limited, mirroring our tendency towards dualistic thought. Such concepts are also, inevitably, based upon the prevailing views of society. Sigmund Freud, for example, was working with men and women whose sexuality was coloured by the morals and mores of the 19th century. Unfortunately, psychologists tend to

explain the higher by contrasting it with the lower: human behaviour is attributed to biological drives, while spirituality is allocated to the unconscious. Sexuality is then seen as an animalistic and base instinct which must be controlled, 'understood', and ultimately neutralized as a 'problem'. Sexuality, therefore, is not seen or accepted as part of life as a whole – but banished to a dark place where it is dissected and limited at best, demonized at worst. And this is both sad and life-denying, for 'All That Is vibrates with desire… the denial of desire will bring you only listlessness. Those who deny desire are the most smitten by it' (Jane Roberts, *The Nature of the Psyche: Its Human Expression).*

We know that most holistic and reverential attitudes towards sexuality were evident in the earliest cultures. In many ways it seems that we have degenerated from an initial state of integration with nature, rather than ascended through some kind of Darwinian evolutionary process. We are constantly told that we represent the apex of human development and evolution, but our sexuality – the engine and energy source of life – is misunderstood, trivialized and negated. It becomes harder and harder to accept that the civilization we see around us is highly evolved. Sex is now big business, but the models of sexuality presented to us are often vicious and demeaning. Sacred consciousness has been lost, warped and distorted. Our natural ability to delight in our senses has also suffered to the extent that an affectionate touch may be perceived solely as a sexual invitation, or intrusion. Both our senses and our spiritual instincts are starved, our notions of sexuality focused on the mechanics of technique and position.

Within such narrow confines relationships are poisoned, creativity stifled, and joyful pleasures rendered suspect. *Sacred Sexuality* offers an alternative to this dreary state of affairs. It is our task to present earlier visions of the magic, beauty and spirituality of sexuality – and to restore sexuality as a sacred art.

When we use the word 'sacred' we mean that which has a common root in the life of the soul and spiritual vision, rather than a reference to religious forms. We believe that spirituality is a dynamic expression of the human psyche. Fundamentally, this remains independent of forms, but seeks expression in and through the world of form. Spiritual forms reflect a sense of the divine in our individual feelings and culture.

The foundations of sacred sexuality are embedded in symbolism. The primary creation myths of all cultures, the gods and goddesses, and the survival of these myths in customs, mysteries and rituals, all symbolize the basic interaction between universal feminine and masculine energies. In many cultures it was self-evident that the primary forces of creativity were initially female and male. Sometimes the male came from the female, on other occasions the female came from the male. Commonly, the sky was seen as male and the earth as female; sunlight as male and moonlight as female; movement as male, receptivity as female. The gods, too, were by no means always male. In the earliest cultures there were active, even aggressive, female deities who had many lovers. As cultural values ebbed and flowed, different myths dominated – sometimes male orientated, sometimes female. When such shifts occurred they were inevitably described as sexual relationships, whether as a result of a desire to integrate, or a need to submit to a conquering tribe.

The male/female, upper/lower polarities are expressed in many powerful ways – such as the Yin/Yang symbol, the sun and moon, the *coniunctio* (sacred marriage) of the alchemical king and queen. In every case it was seen as the coupling of the two most powerful forces in the universe. This union created the world, and everything in it – and provided a model for human integration. It is clear that not only must the two polar energies come together in the outer world, but that we must also integrate these principles within our most private selves and our relationships.

Today, the mechanism of polarity is a central tenet in both science and psychology. The initial energy of the universe polarizes into myriad forms, but when the duality disappears – as it must – only one reality remains. In our physical brains this polarity can be seen in the left and right hemispheres. Synchronizing these two sides is a fundamental goal of consciousness expansion, and meditation in all its forms. Indeed, the left and right halves of the brain have been likened to the male (linear and timebound) and female (lateral and timeless) qualities. The feeling of unity and transcendence we experience in our most ecstatic moments is most often first glimpsed through sexual activity. When we sense the unity of love, we are filled with the desire to overcome the lonely restrictions of duality.

To early cultures the fundamental mechanisms of the universe were seen as reflections of a divine female/male polarity. In modern times our concept of ecology has begun to acknowledge the idea of a living earth. Scientist James Lovelock's Gaia hypothesis presents the idea of our planet as a sentient organism – a radical idea which has rapidly gained credence and acceptance – perhaps because it resonates so profoundly with our instinctive sense of the life-force in all things. Such ideas are manifestations of an ancient drama. We have seen it as essentially human, but it is universal; it is a need to join earth with heaven, both physically and spiritually, to reunite the whole.

In this book our primary concern is with cultures in which sexuality had, or still has, a sacred dimension – if only amongst a few individuals or initiates. Many traditions understood and utilized the sacred nature of sexuality, creating personal patterns, collective rituals and magical techniques. These honoured and celebrated sexuality as a powerful tool for spiritual enlightenment, personal growth, and ecstatic vision. As we shall see, these myths and their accompanying art, rituals, and poetry present vibrant and compelling images. They are images of a dream, a vision, whose goal is unity. Our collective psyche seeks both unity and transcendence. Collectively, then, we must strive to heal ourselves. We must restore our sacred sexuality. In Goethe's words:

> *Whatever you can do,*
> *Or dream you can do,*
> *Begin it.*
> *Boldness has genius, power*
> *   and magic in it.*
> *Begin it now.*

A T MANN AND JANE LYLE

ABOVE *The Bride and Groom (Les Mariés) by Marc Chagall (1887–1985). The portrayal of Adam and Eve continues to the present day but the ideal relationship that they previously represented has changed substantially and is increasingly being questioned and challenged.*

CHAPTER 1

In the Beginning

RIGHT *Eve, the Serpent and Death by Hans Baldung Grien (1484/5– 1545). The serpent is often equated with Death, showing its lineage as a primary symbol of the Earth Mother or Goddess who bestows life but also takes it away.*

> YOU ARE THE TREE OF KNOWLEDGE, WHICH IS IN PARADISE, FROM WHICH THE FIRST MAN ATE, AND WHICH OPENED HIS MIND, SO THAT HE BECAME ENAMOURED OF HIS CO-LIKENESS.
>
> *'On the Origin of the World'*[1]

Although the myth of Adam and Eve existed a thousand years before Christ, for many it is accepted (sometimes literally) as the origin of humanity in the world and the primary archetype of the male/female relationship. The Bible is characteristically patriarchal: God the creator is male and makes the first human in his own image, with Eve being created from Adam's rib as an afterthought. The woman is thus portrayed as secondary and inferior to the man. This doctrine, which places men in control and women in subjugation, is central to Judeo-Christian religion and has also had a profound effect on attitudes to sex and sexuality.

An alternative creation story was revealed in a Gnostic scripture found at Nag Hammadi in Egypt in 1945. Known as 'On the Origin of the World', the text is composed of Hellenistic, Christian, Gnostic, Hebrew, Egyptian and Coptic magical and philosophical themes. These demonstrated that the first man and woman embodied transcendent and sacred principles and that the creation of these two separate beings symbolized a parting from an initial divine unity. To become one again and regain this unity was seen as the secret and essential function of relationship and sexuality.

Gnosticism was an early Christian mystical movement which integrated Jewish and oriental knowledge (*gnosis*) with hidden traditions. Gnostic texts were included in early versions of the Bible, but because of their radical mysticism were excluded when Christianity was accepted by Constantine in the 4th century AD. The Gnostic myth of Adam and Eve in the Garden of Eden is very different from the traditional version of Genesis – and not only for its paradoxical language and the circular reasoning of Gnostic thought. It reveals a doctrine of equality between the sexes which had existed in early Middle Eastern religions, but which had been superseded by both the Hebrew fathers before Christ and the Christian Church in the centuries after Christ, until it was eventually eradicated altogether. The most profound difference in the Gnostic version of creation is that Adam and Eve were hermaphroditic – they each carried male and female qualities. Also, the primary creative force in their coming-into-being was seen as the female principle (found in many myths) rather than the action of a patriarchal god.

According to the Gnostic text, the boundless one, Pistis (faith), appeared as a heavenly likeness of herself in Sophia (wisdom) to veil the light of the cosmos from the void of Chaos. A manifestation of her shadow arose as a spiritless and androgynous ruler, lion-like in appearance, from within the primordial waters (which symbolize the swirling, fecund formlessness of space, or what we would call the unconscious). This ruler, Ariael, who came to be known as the First Father, believed himself to be alone in creation because Pistis/Sophia had withdrawn up into her light. The First Father

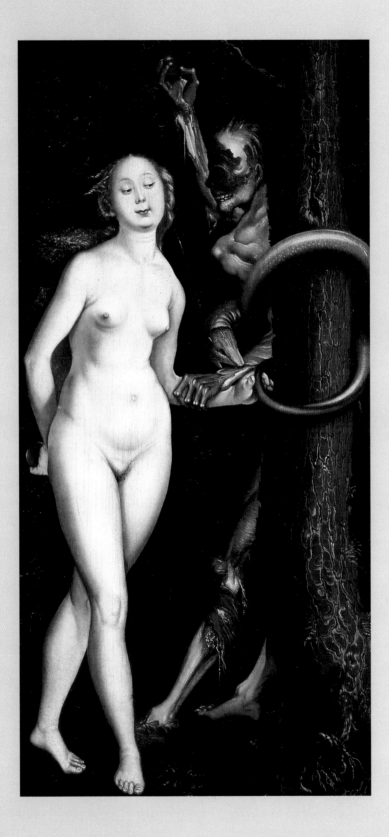

ABOVE *Head of Eros (Vatican Museum). Eros the hermaphroditic god/dess was represented as being a beautiful youth in Roman mythology.*

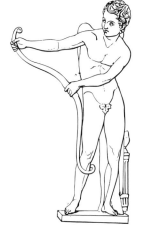

ABOVE *Eros Trying His Bow (Capitoline Museum). The Romans transformed Eros into the god of love and friendship between youths and men, and he therefore was portrayed in his male guise and generally placed in gymnasia between Hermes and Hercules.*

RIGHT *Sophia by Caroline Smith. Sophia is the ancient goddess of wisdom, considered an attribute of the feminine principle.*

saw only himself, and his word appeared as a spirit moving over the waters. He divided the water from the dry land, created heaven and earth, and produced seven androgynous rulers to govern the regions of heaven, and the other gods and demons. Ariael told all the gods, 'I am God. No other exists except me.' But, acting recklessly, he demanded that if any other gods existed before him they should show their light. And he saw the light from Pistis/Sophia above, and became extremely jealous.

Eros came into being from the attraction between the First Father and Sophia, appearing out of the watery midpoint of light and darkness. Eros was androgynous – his masculine being was fire from the light, and his feminine nature was the blood of the virgin. (S)he was handsome and beautiful and everyone who saw Eros became so enamoured that the Eros-flame came to exist in all the gods and creatures of creation, and sexual desire was awakened upon the earth. And Paradise was created, in the centre of which grew the Tree of Knowledge and of Life, followed by all vegetation and the variety of creatures that populate the earth. In all these species of beings,

the desire to mate originated in the principle of Eros. The first Psyche (soul) loved Eros and poured her blood upon him and the earth, from which the rose sprouted out of the thorn bush. And the world was ready to receive man.

Sophia floated a divine drop of light upon the waters, from which, after 12 months' gestation the first man emerged. But he had been created within a woman of Sophia's own female image – Eve. She was the first virgin, not having a husband, and her son was the spiritual Light-Adam who is the lord. She said of herself,

I am the woman,
and I am the virgin.
My husband is the one who begot me,
and I am his mother,
and he is my father and my lord.
I am still in a nascent state,
but I have borne a lordly man.[2]

LEFT *Eros in Flight (Hellenistic terracotta figurine, c 150–100 BC). A figurine made at Myrina in Asia Minor shows the god of love whose function was to seduce all creatures, male and female.*

Because the seven rulers were afraid that Adam would learn to rule his body, he was born with no soul, but after 40 days Eve breathed a soul into him.[3] When Adam arose and saw her, he said, 'You will be called the mother of the living, because you are the one who gave me life.' The rulers were so disturbed that she had animated Adam that they maliciously cast him into a stupor, and in his sleep taught him that Eve had come into being from his rib and that she would serve him and he would rule over her. The immortal Eve laughed at the rulers' false intentions and darkened their eyes. She then left a physical likeness of her body next to Adam, but her spirit entered the Tree of Knowledge and she became the tree. The rulers recklessly cast their seed upon the likeness, and this physical Eve bore the sons and daughters of man.

Adam and Eve were blind in their ignorance of good and evil, eating from the bountiful trees in Eden, but the rulers warned them not to eat from the Tree of Knowledge, on penalty of death. However, the beast of Paradise (the wisest of creatures and spiritual vehicle of the immortal Eve) instructed the physical Eve not to be afraid, and told her that the tree's fruit would enable her and Adam to become like gods and know the distinctions between good and evil. It also said that the rulers had warned them not to eat the fruit only because they were jealous. So Eve and Adam ate from the tree and saw the distinctions between good and evil, but were forever cast out of Paradise.

♦ ♦ ♦

THE SPLIT OF HEAVEN FROM EARTH

♦ ♦ ♦

It was natural to the Gnostic mind that Adam and Eve should be earthly and animalistic even though they were derived from spiritual light. In the Gnostic story of creation, the principles of heaven and earth, male and female, become so completely enmeshed that it is impossible to separate them. It is made very clear that we carry both principles within us. In the Gnostic gospels, each generation of godlike or earthly male and female beings comes together again in the act of reproduction: the first off-spring is hermaphrodite, and then there is a differentiation into male and female. The process repeats endlessly, both on spiritual and terrestrial levels. What is fascinating is that this ancient view of conception also occurs in human biology. Due to the genetic mechanism, we are all initially female until males develop male qualities and differentiate themselves from the primarily female ovum.

The rejection of Gnostic teachings in favour of the patriarchal view was a turning point in the development of Western religion, philosophy and sacred sexuality. We are told that we are created by an omnipotent and perfect God, who remains above and beyond His mortal creations. But according to the Gnostic vision, the male creators of the world were envious, malevolent and out of control. Our legacy from the Judeo-Christian view is a hierarchy of male over female, differentiation between the sexes, and a cover-up of the truth about the spiritual origins of sexuality. As a result we have become divided beings, which makes us mortal and finite, and is the 'original sin' for which we can never atone.

It is clear that the traditional biblical story was specifically designed to eliminate equality between the sexes, and to repress and depotentize any powerful influences remaining from the cults of the Earth Mother, or Great Goddess, which had ruled supreme for tens of thousands of years.

The myth of the first woman and man in Paradise is powerful because it carries universal validity as an 'archetype'. This was defined by Carl Jung as a dominant but invisible structure in the psyche that takes specific form when it emerges into consciousness.[4] Such unconscious structures are universal aspects of human behaviour and consciousness and condition our behaviour and beliefs. The Gnostic myth expresses the duality we carry as our Western psychological heritage, expressed in magical terms.

Sexual intercourse was condemned as an evil act in early Christian times, despite the fact that priestly celibacy was not instituted until many centuries later. It was believed that when the Eros principle arose, marriage between man and woman ensued, followed by reproduction and eventually death. Sexuality therefore was equated with death, and as sexual desires inevitably led to mortality, sex was considered a sin, although this view disallowed the possibility of spirituality and the transcendence of sexuality.

The elimination of the female within the male led inexorably to soullessness, and it was not until the mystical Hebrew literature of the Kabbala a thousand years later that the mystical Adam rejoined the Tree of Life.

It is fascinating that the Gnostic beast of Paradise – also seen as a snake or serpent, and identified both with spirituality and with Eve – is considered to be the key to wisdom in Eden, yet in its snake form it is always portrayed in Christian teachings as devilish and evil.

The feminine principle is here presented as evil rather than wisdom, and it is the jealous patriarchal gods who are enthroned. (In oriental mythologies the snake does not carry such a freight of symbolic evil; it symbolizes the creative force of the world, corresponding to the *kundalini* energy that spirals around the spinal column, and is a primary symbol of the Great Goddess.) Sexuality, therefore, can be seen as a force for either wisdom or ignorance, depending on which teachings are followed.

RIGHT *Eros as Genius of
Death (Vatican). Eros was
born from Chaos at the
same time as Earth and
Tartarus, and was conceived
by the historian Hesiod as
the power that forms the
world by the inner union of
separated elements.*

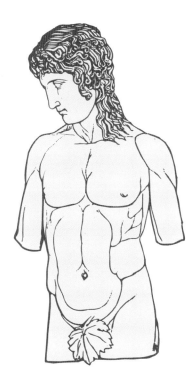

CHAPTER 2

Serpent Goddess

ABOVE *Artemis/Diana of Ephesus (2nd century BC Ephesus). The Greek Artemis and Roman Diana carried on the earlier symbolism of the Anatolian mother goddess Cybele. She is associated with the zodiac sign Sagittarius as the huntress and appears with many breasts as an Earth Mother.*

Before the dawn of civilization some 5,000 years ago, cults devoted to the Great Goddess or Earth Mother had been worshipping for tens of thousands of years. The core of these cults was the magical worship of fertility, sexuality and death. The dynamic of male/female relationships was the core of that magic. Being unaware of the biological mechanisms of procreation, paleolithic and neolithic peoples imagined a great diversity of fantastic ways to explain the fundamental facts of human existence and the cycles of nature which surrounded and sustained them. Their world was sacred and they were subject to powerful cosmic forces, which they visualized as a realm populated by gods and goddesses and totemic beings under whose control they lived and died. Everything in the world, visible and hidden, was animated by these all-powerful deities, and their worship constituted the primary structure of society.[5]

They regarded sexual intercourse as the ultimate magical act, and in its thrall they entered the domain and blind power of the gods and goddesses. For them fertility was not a path to spiritual integration because they were already at one with their spirit world. Fertility required sacrifice: failure to propagate, to find animals for food, or to ensure fertility led to death. In these cults the Great Mother symbolized life itself. In the earliest known cult figurines the goddess was shown as a heavy- or many-breasted woman baring the source of her sexual energy.

One of the primary symbols of the early Great Mother cults of neolithic times was the cosmic serpent.[6] The goddess's temples contained snakes, and in some images of her they are coiled around her body or clenched in her upraised arms. She was sometimes shown as a serpent with the head of a goddess.

The symbolism of the serpent in Earth Mother cultures is important, and the transformation of this symbolism over the years reflects the disappearance of the goddess religions in the wake of patriarchal religions and beliefs. The snake is a symbol of eternal life and reincarnation because of the way it periodically sheds its skin. The snake/dragon symbolizes the cosmic waters, darkness, that which is hidden, the unformed, the amorphous and the virtual, all of which are associated with the realm of the Earth Mother goddess.[7] The snake disappears into holes in the ground or murky waters, leaving the domain of life for its dark journey into the underworld and into communion with the spirits which reside there.

In Indian myth the serpent kings and queens *(nāgas)* personify the waters of lakes, rivers and oceans, which are controlled by the moon.[8] A snake is often seen curled round the world egg, a symbol of generation and the mystery of life which, when halved, is like the vault of the heavens. The spiralling snake, symbolizes both the spontaneous life energy contained in the created universe and the cyclical nature of all life on earth. This powerful image refers to the essential nature of the goddess who, although mainly associated with birth, is also mistress of death and the underworld.

The snake was a primary component of healing rituals, such as those which took place in the circular Tholos temple at the sanctuary of the Greek healing god Asclepius at Epidaurus. The temple

Goddess Kali seated in intercourse with the double corpse of Shiva (19th century Punjab). Over the life force of Shiva the dark goddess Kali is dominant, showing that the god of life is in connection with both his consort Shakti as the eternal feminine and the conception which leads to death and rebirth. Here this dual nature is shown.

RIGHT *Coiled Hindu Nāga serpent (7th–8th century Andhra Pradesh). The Nāga serpent ruled the underworld because snakes live on the ground in holes leading into the darkness below, paralleling their symbolism of the sexual act.*

foundations contained circular channels, which almost certainly contained live snakes, making it a reservoir of powerful healing energy upon which the physician priests/priestesses could draw. Patients slept in a specially oriented building, around and upon which snakes were free to crawl. Their dreams were believed to provide a cure for their sickness, and if touched by a snake, a cure was assured. A remnant of this powerful and ancient process remains in the caduceus, the winged staff with snakes entwined around it, which is to this day the emblem of the medical profession.

Above, the Great Mother Serpent of Heaven constellation encircled the pole-star.[9] Early cultures identified the serpent's movement around the pole-star with the cycle of the constellations in the astrological year. It also acted as the pointer for the precession of the equinoxes, showing the progress of the earth's polar axis as it appeared to wander around the pole-star. This movement created the astrological Great Year, as the precessional movement backwards through the zodiac signs determined the transitions between the times when the aeons changed. The backward movement of the precession contradicted the masculine sun's forward movement around the seasonal zodiac circle and was therefore associated with the feminine. There is still a strong association between the right-hand path and the

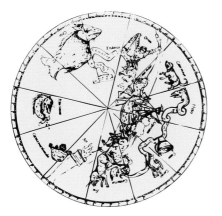

masculine nature and the left-hand path with the feminine, both in magic and sacred sexuality.

As the sun appeared to move forward through the zodiac, the lunar goddess rose earlier and earlier each night until she disappeared for three days around the time of the new moon, during which time she 'died' and was reborn. The backward movement of the moon and the precession was identified with the feminine influence of the serpent. It contained mystery and darkness and untold power. The serpent carried this eternal cosmic message and evoked powerful worship.

The points where the moon's path crossed the ecliptic of the zodiacal planetary movements were called the dragon's head and dragon's tail, and they were seen as places where her energy entered or left the earth's plane. Some of the earliest stone monuments of lunar goddess cultures were oriented in order to predict the times of eclipses, which are determined by the 18.67-year Metonic cycle movement of the nodes,[10] the time separating eclipses falling in the exact degrees of the zodiac and on the same day of the year. The serpent goddesses were thus active guides to all aspects of early life on our planet.

♦ ♦ ♦
SKY GOD AND MOTHER EARTH
♦ ♦ ♦

Woman was identified with the Earth Mother through her fertility, her power over the dragon and serpent forces that determined the cycles of time, and because she traversed the inner worlds of creation, sexuality and death. She was parthenogenic, able to conceive and give birth to offspring on her own, and was powerful enough to do this without the help of the gods, just as her magical powers enabled her to influence the growth of plants for food. As a primary part of Earth Mother worship, her priestesses made love in the fields to ensure fertility.

The correlation of the Great Goddess with the moon and its mysterious movements supported these ideas. The moon became a smaller and smaller crescent until she vanished for three days, but she always reappeared, as though she had created herself from the darkness to regain her place in the evening sky. The fact that the cycle of the moon in the sky echoed the menstrual rhythms of women – the wounds which always healed – reinforced the correlation.

LEFT *The constellation Hydra, the serpent, appears to move around the northern pole-star and serves as a pointer for the precession of the equinoxes, the astrological world ages (18th-century engraving).*

BELOW *Tholos Sanctuary sacred to Asklepios at Epidaurus by Polycleitus (360–320 BC). The healing sanctuary of the Greek healing god, Asklepios, was circular, reflecting its function of achieving wholeness. Underneath it were ranged concentric rings of pits in which it is thought the snakes which were integral to the healing rituals were kept.*

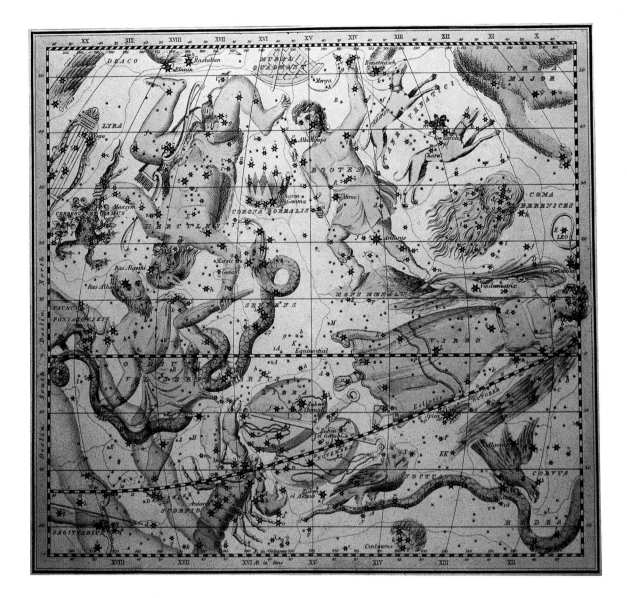

ABOVE *Celestial Chart of the Heavens showing Autumn zodiac signs and astrological instruments (engraved by John Emslie 1813–1875). The skies were saturated with symbolism carried by the constellations, awaiting their reception on earth below.*

Mother Earth was the power that brought life to humanity in the natural world. She was omnipotent, and thus she had little need for male influence in her world.

The Great Goddess had many names: to the Greeks she was known as Mother Earth, Demeter, Rhea, Aphrodite, Potnia, Selene, Pallas Athena in her bird and snake goddess form rather than her later Amazonian type, Gaia and Cybele; to the Babylonians she was Astarte or Ishtar, while to the Egyptians she was Isis and Hathor. Later her influence continued through more abstract names which none the less signified her power – the Star of the Night, Lady of the Night, the Dark Goddess, the Black Virgin – or in even more subtle forms such as the Hebrew spirit, which is feminine, and

LEFT *Inca Madonna*
(Spanish school 17th
century)

the Christian Holy Ghost.[11] She was also the Greek *pneuma*, meaning spirit, the Hindu *prana*, meaning vital force or breath, and the Gnostic Sophia, meaning wisdom. Her Eastern manifestations occurred in many forms, each signifying an aspect of her energies and powers. As a goddess she was known as Kali, Shakti or *dakini* (female carrier of the demonic energy of wisdom), and as Durga, the goddess of ecstatic and orgiastic sexual rites.

When the Great Goddess was associated with the moon, she possessed a quality which could only be called 'black'. The moon gradually changes appearance throughout her monthly lunar cycle, and these periods of association were seen as times of death, disintegration and evil darkness. Therefore

RIGHT *Hindu Black Goddess Durga (8th–9th century). Durga was the goddess of ecstatic sexual rites and of the destructive aspect which came into being through the lives created as a result of sexual abandon.*

many of the goddesses also had shadow sides, which terrified even the brave. In these forms she was goddess of the underworld (as Hecate or Persephone) or the black Hindu goddess Kali. 'O Shiva! Please reveal the inner meaning of my mystic form as Kali, she who is black as the limitless night sky, awesome, fearful, yet compassionate.'[12] In Hindu representations, she was shown as the bottom-most point of the downward-

pointing triangle of the goddesses, together with Lakshmi (preserving Divine Energy) and Saraswati (creative Divine Energy), showing that she was the deepest and darkest aspect of the divine female. As the Hindu goddess Durga she was the black virgin.

Many of her manifestations were parthenogenic, because she was able to reproduce herself, and she therefore shared names which mean 'virgin' as well as 'whore'. She was unavailable or hidden, but also came out of herself in the sexual rites of frenzy, during which she exposed everything. The Babylonian goddess Ishtar was known as 'Heavenly Prostitute' as well as 'Virgin'. In many cultures the goddess as the Great Mother was the protector of virgins, but simultaneously the patroness of prostitutes. There always seemed to be an inter-mingling of her forms. (In this context the term 'virgin' was associated more with the concept of a 'divine female', than a woman who has never made love.)[13]

RIGHT *Lunar Goddess Ishtar (2100–2000 BC Ur III Period). Ishtar, whose symbol is the crescent moon, introduces the governor of a city to the King of Ur. Ancient kings needed the support of the lunar goddess, symbolizing their victory over matriarchy and chaos.*

Worship of the Great Mother was not only a spiritual phenomenon; it also formed the foundation of numerous sects, rituals and cultural customs. In later patriarchal cultures the serpent began to take on other meanings. It came to symbolize male potency as the phallus, although it was created within the goddess and after performing its functions returned to sleep there curled up in her embrace. This again echoes the lives of snakes which return to their caves under the ground to restore their energies. Ultimately the snake became a primary symbol of male sexual energy.

♦ ♦ ♦
CONQUERING THE DRAGON
♦ ♦ ♦

Just as the serpent had represented the Great Goddess and Earth Mother, so later cultures symbolized the rise of masculine influence by myths of heroes conquering the dragon. It was believed that the dragon must be killed and cut into pieces by the gods in order to bring birth to the cosmos, as in the myth relating the death and dismemberment of the Egyptian Osiris by Set (time). In Babylonia, the sun god Marduk created

ABOVE *Full Moon and Sun Set by Caroline Smith. The relationship between masculine sun and feminine moon is a prototype of creation. When the female principle is dominant it is like the setting sun.*

ABOVE *St Michael,
Signorelli (1500, Rome).
St Michael is often shown
with scales in his hand as
the Lord of Souls, an
image like those in the
Egyptian Book of the
Dead.*

RIGHT *St George and
the Dragon by Paolo
Uccello (1397–1475). A
classical representation of
the hero killing the dragon
and saving the maiden. It
is thought to represent the
hero conquering the
unconscious chaos, but also
symbolizes male
domination of earlier
goddess cults (represented
by the dragon). There is
the additional implication
of woman as passive and in
need of salvation by the
hero / father. The armour of
the hero protects him not
only from the dragon, but
also from the danger of
sexuality, seen as the
province of woman.*

the world from the body of the sea
monster Tiamat (who symbolized the
primordial timeless world) by slicing up
his body to make the yearly calendar and
its twelve zodiac signs.[14]

Early Christian legends depict
St Michael and St George killing a
dragon, apparently to rid the pure
Christians of primeval menace. But in
reality they were both identified with
Church fathers who were intent on
extinguishing the earlier Great Goddess
cults, and replacing them with the
Christian Church. Naturally, many of
the churches dedicated to these saints are
located on sites previously sacred to
the Earth Mother, and at intersections
of the ley lines (dragon lines) which
criss-cross the British countryside, such
as on Glastonbury Tor.[15]

The victory of the gods over the
dragon at the beginning of time was
never permanent – it needed to be ritually repeated every year, just as the sun
god was reborn every year at the winter
solstice (like Christ) and the world was
recreated once again. The ascendancy
over darkness, chaos and death, as symbolized by the dragon, was a central
motif in the mythologies of virtually all
cultures where the goddess was banished
to the underworld and replaced by patriarchal beliefs. Subsequently, when such
cultures experienced a breakdown of
order or a loss in battle, it was assumed
that the mythic dragon had returned to
rebel against the order instilled by the
gods. In our age this process happens
psychologically, within us, and is
nowhere expressed as powerfully as in
our sexuality.

CHAPTER 3

Descent of the Feminine

THERE CAME A TIME WHEN
THE GODDESS WAS NO LONGER
WORSHIPPED; THEN THE
PHYSICAL AND SPIRITUAL
ASPECTS OF THE FEMININE
WERE DECLARED EVIL.[16]

FOR TO AVOID BEING LURED
INTO THE SNARE OF LOVE IS
NOT SO DIFFICULT AS, WHEN
YOU ARE CAUGHT IN THE
TOILS, TO GET OUT AND BREAK
THROUGH THE STRONG
KNOTS OF VENUS.[17]

RIGHT *Painting by Arthur Hacker (1858–1919) showing the timeless links between women and nature*

It had to happen. The collective pendulum swung, and what had once been elevated, revered and, above all, celebrated, fell spectacularly from grace. There are numerous theories and controversial hypotheses that offer reasons for this great sea-change. Briefly, their main arguments can be summarized in the following way:
♦ The matriarchal and matrilineal basis of society became both patriarchal and patrilineal.
♦ Agricultural societies developed and began to trade with other cultures. As they explored the world they became acquisitive, and this invariably led to invasions and wars. Aggressive, powerful father gods gained ground, usurping the feminine deities who had once been fearsome warrior queens as well as sensual goddesses of love.[18]
♦ Women, who had been the sole guardians and creators of life and were therefore mysterious and awesome beings, lost a great deal of their power when men realized they were also responsible for creating babies. The real-

ization of paternity prompted spiritual and material changes in men.

*In woman are incarnated
the disturbing mysteries of nature,
and man escapes her hold when
he frees himself from nature.*

SIMONE DE BEAUVOIR, THE SECOND SEX.

During the millennia which saw the development of politics, war, and commerce, the role of women became ever less important in the overall scheme of things. The image of the Great Goddess and her consort was replaced by a wider spectrum of male and female divinities, many with overlapping rulerships. Eventually, and not without a struggle, masculine monotheism triumphed. There was now one male god who thundered, 'Thou shalt have no other gods before me.' Feminine sexuality continued to be acknowledged as a potent

LEFT *The Baths of Caracalla (1899), by Sir Lawrence Alma Tadema (1836–1912). Victorian fantasies about women's sexuality were the inspiration for numerous paintings.*

ABOVE *Odalisque à l'esclave by Ingres. Eastern cultures symbolized sensuality in 19th-century Europe.*

FAR RIGHT *William Blake's visionary image of God as an all-powerful patriarch has remained an archetypal symbol into the present day.*

force — it would take the Victorians to perceive women as entirely passive vessels — but instead of being universally venerated, it was eventually seen as the reason for all mankind's troubles. Woman became a symbolic and actual temptation to be resisted, and even degraded. The old belief that sensual pleasures were divine gifts and could lead to a state of spiritual grace was seen to be inextricably associated with goddess worship. This was anathema to patriarchal religion, so it came to be ruthlessly suppressed: temples were destroyed and celibacy, martyrdom and masochistic mortification of the flesh became theological ideals.

♦ ♦ ♦
PHILOSOPHERS AND PATRIARCHS
♦ ♦ ♦

The origins of this orgy of misogyny lay in Classical Greece, where women's roles in relation to men were clearly delineated by Demosthenes: 'Man has the courtesan for erotic enjoyment, concubines for daily use, and wives of his own rank to bring up his children and be faithful housewives.'

Roman philosophers expanded upon the dualism inherent in the first division of heaven and earth. Heaven, intellect, and spiritual qualities were identified as positive masculine principles, while

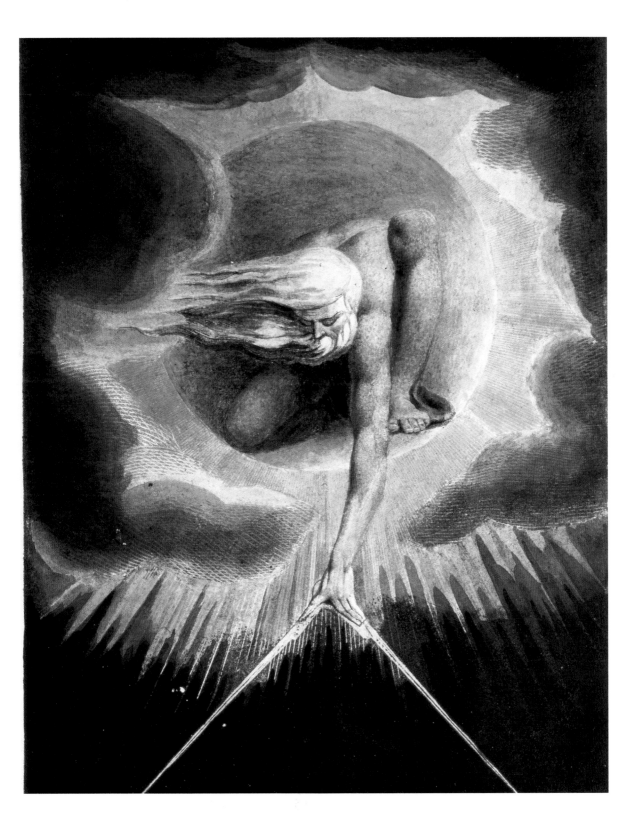

earth, fertility and physicality were identified as negative feminine principles. In the beginning, a fruitful marriage took place between the two but eventually they became warring factions, with the earthy empire of the senses fated to be the loser.

The pernicious split between the symbolic Virgin, or good woman, and the Whore, or bad woman, has its origins in this earlier breakup. According to the Virgin/Whore fantasy, a good woman is a bloodless creature. She overflows with traditional virtues such as patience, honesty, and kindness. She is also pure and chaste and never disturbed by the unruly promptings of sexual desire, nor does she take pleasure in the act of sexual intercourse. These attributes deny her womanhood, creating a non-threatening partner for the male. He need never worry that she might leave him or betray him with another, since she finds no joy in sex. But a woman's body is designed for sensual pleasure. The clitoris, for example, has no other function, for this small bud of flesh is packed with sensitive nerve endings which respond to caresses. In some parts of the world the clitoris is still surgically removed to prevent women experiencing orgasms. However, mutual sexual pleasure is a magical and compelling experience for both partners.

Rather than deny this altogether, the Virgin is forever joined with her opposite number, the Whore. Sexual pleasure may still be experienced with this figure, but it is split off from 'the love of a good woman' since – as the theory goes – good women know nothing of carnal enjoyment. Whores embody the sexual feminine, the independent woman, the dark and dangerous realms of ecstasy. Therefore, the fantasy tells us, she is bad and can lead men astray by tempting them into her bed. The pleasures they experience there are tainted by sin, but since she seduced them, they are not responsible and may easily repent. This dual image of the feminine has no corresponding male archetype. A good man is not necessarily a celibate saint, and a bad man may be a faithful husband.

The Virgin/Whore split remains a fantasy, but one which still wields a certain amount of influence today.

Historically, this way of thinking took root over many centuries. Tertullian (150–230 AD), for example, wrote that 'Woman is a temple over a sewer', and suggested that women should dress in mourning clothes to show how sorry they were for having caused the fall of the entire human race. Needless to say, women failed to comply with his wishes. Men such as Plotinus (3rd century AD) promoted the creed of sexual and sensual repression as a way to God, but the greatest and most enduring influence evolved from the teachings of St Paul and St Augustine.

It is good for a man not
to touch a woman. Nevertheless,
to avoid fornication, let every man have
his own wife. But if they have not
continency, let them marry,
for it is better to marry than to burn.

ST PAUL, CORINTHIANS 7:1–2

BELOW *La Grande Odalisque by Ingres. For centuries the sexual feminine was embodied by courtesans and prostitutes.*

RIGHT *Eve, blamed
for the fall of mankind,
nonetheless inspired
countless paintings. This
knowing version is by
Hans Baldung Grien.*

*I know nothing which
brings the manly mind down
from the heights more than
a woman's caresses and
that joining of bodies without
which one cannot have a wife.*

ST AUGUSTINE

The thoughts, words and deeds of these
two moral heavyweights ushered in centuries of repression and its inevitable
companion, hypocrisy – for in the real
world people continued to fall in love
and experience all the joys and torments

of desire. The Eastern branch of the
Church and the Celtic Christians both
went their own merrier ways, ignoring
for the most part the dreary, life-denying
edicts of the early Church fathers. In
England, for example, it was more than a
thousand years before Christian priests
were officially required to be celibate.
Thereafter many scandals enlivened
monastic and clerical life when neither
the flesh nor the spirit was willing or
able to comply with the doctrine of
complete chastity.

Ironically, the original wording of the
Anglican marriage vows was based on an
older Anglo-Saxon tradition. The suspi-
ciously pagan promise 'with my body I
thee worship' was somehow retained. In
the Anglo-Saxon version the bridegroom vowed: 'With this ring I thee
wed, and this gold and silver I give thee,
and with my body I thee worship, and
with all my worldly chattels I thee
honour.' His bride then replied: 'I take
thee to my wedded husband, to have and
to hold, for fairer for fouler, for better
for worse, for richer for poorer, in sickness and in health, to be bonny and
buxom in bed and at board, till death us
do part.'[19]

♦ ♦ ♦

EVE'S CURSE

♦ ♦ ♦

*Unto the woman he said,
I will greatly multiply thy sorrow
and thy conception;
in sorrow thou shalt bring
forth children; and thy desire
shall be to thy husband,
and he shall rule over thee.*

GENESIS 3:16

The biblical curse borne by Eve and all her daughters represents a neat reversal of the beliefs and practices sacred to the goddess. It is central to all the dogma and doctrine that followed, and led to 'The proliferation of guilt, trapping human beings in an endless cycle of sin-and-repentance … the cultural legacy of the Dark Ages of early Christianity. Western society is only now beginning to crawl out of its shadow.'[20]

The God of the Judeo-Christian tradition says he will multiply her conception, thus threatening women's knowledge of birth control and the tantric secrets of withholding ejaculation, which are more fully explored in Chapter 6. Eve is also threatened with labour pains, something priestesses and midwives with their extensive knowledge of herbs knew how to alleviate. Such curses and the lambasting of midwives were attempts to curb the potency of the old ways. The *Malleus Maleficarum* ('The Hammer of Evildoers') 1484, essential reading for witchfinders, said: 'No one does more harm to the Catholic faith than midwives.' Indeed, the word midwife is derived from the

Anglo-Saxon 'med-wyf', meaning wise woman, another term for witch. In 1559 the English Parliamentary Articles of Enquiry urged churchmen to be especially vigilant when faced with 'charms, sorcery, enchantments, invocations, circles, witchcrafts, soothsaying … especially in the time of women's travails.' Even as late as the 19th century the use of painkillers in childbirth was considered a sin against God, and in America chloroform was regarded as 'a decoy of Satan'.

Finally, Eve's sexuality and autonomy are cursed. She must desire only her husband, and submit to his will. Eve's curse neatly disposes of goddess worship, sacred sexual practices and female equality with men in one succinct sentence. In the 12th century, Odo of Cluny echoed Tertullian when he asserted that 'to embrace a woman is to embrace a sack of manure'. The *Malleus Maleficarum*

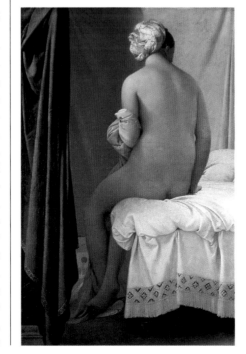

LEFT *Witches, symbolic of the suppressed goddesses of old, were credited with great power and supernatural knowledge.*

LEFT *Another example by Ingres of the sexual feminine, safely contained within the context of a non-Christian culture.*

RIGHT *The infamous witch trials continued for centuries. Those in Salem, America, were among the last manifestations of this hysteria.*

confidently states that: 'All witchcraft comes from carnal lust, which is in women insatiable.' This may stem from an old Arab proverb which appears in the Bible:

*There are three things that are never
satisfied, yea, four things
say not, it is enough:
the grave; and the barren womb;
the earth that is not filled with water;
and the fire that saith not,
it is enough.*

PROVERBS 30:15–16.

Anything that hinted at pagan joys, fertility rituals or sexual freedom was roundly condemned, although this disapproving atmosphere could never eradicate such activities altogether. Pagan customs exuded a vitality with which the Church and State could never compete. Trial marriages, later known as 'living in sin', were a widespread

RIGHT *Witches were believed to make a pact with the Devil. In this picture he carries a witch off to eternal torment.*

phenomenon, especially in more remote districts. As late as the 18th century, men and women underwent a ceremony called handfasting at Lammastide (1 August), when they chose a partner with whom they would live for a year. At the end of that time they decided whether to stay together or part company and choose a new partner. This custom, which evokes the myth of the goddess and her annual consort, was known by a number of names including tarrying, night-visiting, and courting-on-the-bed. Country people were not squeamish in sexual matters, unlike many of the more literate members of society. For example, in the 16th century, Philip Stubbes, a prudish English Puritan, wrote with outraged prurience of the May Eve fertility revels which had taken place in every rural district since time immemorial: 'I have heard it credibly reported by men of great gravity, credit and reputation; that of forty, threescore or a hundred maids going to the wood over night, there have scarcely the third part of them returned home undefiled.'[21]

Meanwhile, in the real world, real women continued to live as mothers, lovers, poets, painters, explorers, pirates, courtesans, merchants, and so on, across the whole spectrum of human activity and endeavour – although often it must have been challenging, to say the least. Little by little, however, human delight in sexuality, the ancient and civilizing arts of contraception and midwifery, and, above all, the spiritual aspects of the feminine principle, were all bundled up together, labelled heretical, and regarded as the exclusive province of Satan. Witches and harlots, visionary women, women who healed and women who lived alone were all persecuted. An inestimable number were hideously tortured and put to death under the grim reign of the Inquisition. This collective hysteria poisoned the European psyche for centuries and later erupted in the notorious witch trials at Salem in America. But the inexorable underground stream flowed on, and sacred sexual secrets – ever more obscurely veiled – made their underground home amidst the songs of the troubadours, alchemical writings, mysterious paintings and sculptures, and at the heart of many Gnostic heresies.

ABOVE *Witches Sabbath by Goya. Like prostitutes, witches were both objects of fascination and revulsion.*

Mesopotamian Holy Harlot

I TURN THE MALE TO THE FEMALE. I AM SHE WHO ADORNETH THE MALE FOR THE FEMALE; I AM SHE WHO ADORNETH THE FEMALE FOR THE MALE.

The words of the goddess Ishtar.

A great and powerful civilization once flourished in Mesopotamia (Greek for 'between the rivers'). This area, now in modern Iraq, included the kingdoms of Sumeria, Akkadia, Assyria and Babylonia, although its culture and influence spread over a much wider area of the Middle East.

The earliest evidence from Sumeria reveals a culture which accorded women equal status with men, and which principally venerated the goddess Inanna/Ishtar, lunar goddess of life and love, named as the Whore of Babylon in the Bible.[22] The Mesopotamians held daily religious rituals, offering food and drink to their deities in the temples – which were also centres for trade and acted as banks, extending loans. Monthly rites were held to honour the moon's phases: 'on the day of the disappearance of the moon, on the day of the sleeping of the moon'. The exact observance of the moon's phases was very important for it formed the calendar from which they calculated the precise dates and times of all their religious observances. The focus and centrepiece of their year was a sacred sexual rite of the utmost significance. Every New Year, the ruling king 'married' the goddess Inanna/Ishtar amidst great feasting and celebration. This rite took place annually for thousands of years,

profoundly influencing later civilizations, both symbolically and through actual ritual.

♦ ♦ ♦

IN PRAISE OF ISHTAR

♦ ♦ ♦

*Praise Ishtar, the most
awesome of the Goddesses,
revere the queen of women,
the greatest of the deities.
She is clothed with pleasure and love.
She is laden with vitality,
charm, and voluptuousness.
In lips she is sweet;
life is in her mouth.
At her appearance rejoicing
becomes full.*[23]

Ishtar's titles and names – like those of all ancient deities – were many and various. In Babylon, her name meant 'Star', the Light of the World. Semitic people gradually conquered the lands of Sumer, introducing changes to the earliest myths and adding further names for the goddess. She was known as Ashtoreth, to whom King Solomon returns at the end of his days; she was also named Har, or Hora – from which the words harlot and whore sprang. Inanna/Ishtar was served by powerful prostitute-priestesses who were 'the vehicles of her creative life in their sexual union with the men who came there to perform a sacred ritual'.[24]

This goddess exhibited a rich diversity of powers, for she also had a terrifying aspect as goddess of war and storms. Her primordial origins are suggested by images depicting her with the magical Tree of Life, the sacred serpent, and numerous birds – linking her with the earliest snake-bird goddesses known to us in many cultures.

Inanna/Ishtar enjoyed many lovers. Her title 'virgin' indicated her autonomous, unmarried state. Her chief consort was the son/brother/lover Dumuzi, or Tammuz, meaning 'faithful son'. This, and the corresponding goddess roles of mother/sister/lover, reflect the phases of the moon, underlining the importance of its monthly cycle to all ancient peoples. Dumuzi/Tammuz is referred to in poems and hymns as 'Lord of Life', 'the Green One', and 'Shepherd of the People' – often sacrificed in the form of a lamb. The other totemic creatures linked to the son/lover are the ram and the magnificent 'Bull of Heaven'.

But, like all early consorts, the grain god Dumuzi/Tammuz was fated to meet an untimely sacrificial end. His ritual death, accompanied by a month of mourning, took place in high summer, after the harvests. This coincided with the reappearance of the dog star, Sirius, rising with the sun in mid-July. At this time, the goddess's lover descended to the 'Land of No Return', the under-world, and life on earth became sterile, scorched and parched by the unforgiving rays of the high summer sun.

The goddess annually mourned the loss of her beloved with piteous laments, intoned by the people in the temples. Naturally, she would eventually retrieve him so that the eternal annual round could be acted out – life affirmed, and life restored. Some scholars suggest that, long ago, an actual human sacrifice took place every Great Year – that is, every eighth year. However, written records did not begin until much later, by which time the death and resurrection of the beloved was acted out symbolically. The god was ever a cyclical deity, while the goddess, like the earth itself, endured. But by the third millennium BC the *Epic of Gilgamesh*[25] had challenged this received wisdom. In this poem Ishtar desires the hero: 'Glorious Ishtar raised an eye at the beauty of Gilgamesh: "Come, Gilgamesh, be thou my lover!

Do but grant me of thy fruit."'

Gilgamesh, however, responds by reciting a long list of Ishtar's previous amours and the sad fate which befell them. He says, 'Which lover didst thou love forever? Which of thy shepherds pleased thee for all time?... For Tammuz, the lover of thy youth, Thou hast ordained wailing year after year...' The hero ultimately rejects the goddess's sexual invitation, slays her divine bull and celebrates his bravura with his friend Enkidu, a savage enemy in another tale. This epic poem clearly reflects gradual changes which were taking place in society at that time, for a male figure not only rejects the great goddess, but triumphs over her furious attempts at revenge.

In other poems, however, the relationship between the goddess and her lover is rapturous, erotic, and burst-ing with images of fertility. Here is the Sumerian Inanna, praising her 'honey-man':

He has sprouted; he has burgeoned;
He is lettuce planted by the water.
He is the one my womb loves best.
My well-stocked garden of the plain,
My barley growing high in its furrow,
My apple tree which bears fruit up to
*   its crown,*
He is lettuce planted by the water.
My honey-man, my honey-man sweetens
*   me always.*
My lord, the honey-man of the gods,
He is the one my womb loves best.
His hand is honey, his foot is honey,
He sweetens me always.
My eager impetuous caresser of the navel,
My caresser of the soft thighs,
He is the one my womb loves best
He is lettuce planted by the water.[26]

RIGHT *A Babylonian alabaster figure of Ishtar*

♦ ♦ ♦
THE WHORES OF BABYLON
♦ ♦ ♦

Ishtar's sacred harlots belonged to an organized hierarchy, painstakingly recorded by the Babylonians. Her top-ranking priestesses were called *entu*, and wore special clothing to distinguish them from the others. Their caps, jewellery and ceremonial staff were the same as those of the ruler, and their status equal to those of the male priests.

The Babylonian *naditu*, ranking next in importance to the entu, were drawn from the highest families in the land. In dedicating their lives to the goddess they were supposed to remain single and childless. However, the naditu cheerfully ignored this stricture, and led full and active lives. They were bright and canny, with considerable business acumen: 'They bought, sold and hired out; lent money and grain; invested, imported, exported, dealt in slaves, managed land and people, played from the cloisters an essential part in the economy of the country.'[27] Beneath these women came the *qadishtu* (sacred women) and the *ishtaritu*, many of whom specialized in the arts of dancing, music and singing.

ABOVE *The snake's sensuous coils may have inspired the undulations of Middle Eastern dance.*

From snippets of information in classical literature, and certain artefacts, it is possible to surmise that these women demonstrated their sexuality by dancing a version of the sensuous, undulating belly dance which is still extremely popular all over the Middle East today. As Wendy Buonaventura writes of the dance: '... everything indicates a connection between birth mime, early creation dance and that which was part of goddess rites in the prehistoric world'. The dance is characterized by 'snake-like and vigorous hip and pelvic movements, the manipulation of veils, a descent to the floor and the ritual wearing of a hip-belt or sash, which we can link with the girdle, Ishtar's symbolic emblem'.[28] In the Middle East this alluring dance is still performed by women, at all-female gatherings from which men are banned.

In addition to the activities of the sacred temple whores, there were sacramental sexual initiations of a slightly different character. The Greek historian Herodotus (3 BC) tells us: 'Babylonian custom... compels every woman of the land once in her life to sit in the temple of love and have intercourse with some stranger... the men pass and make their choice. It matters not what be the sum of money; the woman will never refuse, for that were a sin, the money being by this act made sacred. After their intercourse she has made herself holy in the sight of the goddess and goes away to her home; and thereafter there is no bribe however great that will get her. So then the women that are tall and fair are soon free to depart, but the uncomely have long to wait because they cannot fulfil the law; for some of them remain for three years or four. There is a custom like this in some parts of Cyprus.'[29]

Many of these women returned home to marry and have children. Later Sumerian texts, however, advised against marrying a fully-fledged temple prostitute since she would be too independent, 'besides being accustomed to accepting other men, she would make an unsympathetic and intractable wife'.

Overall, the sacred whores were credited with transformative powers, as the myth of the wild, hairy Enkidu makes plain. The *Epic of Gilgamesh* tells how the semi-divine hero became so overweeningly arrogant that the other gods created Enkidu to steal some of his power. A hunter discovered this primitive being at a watering hole, drinking with the animals, and informed Gilgamesh of the trap. On hearing the news, Gilgamesh sent a 'child of pleasure' from the temple of love to lure Enkidu away. The woman disrobed, 'laying bare her ripeness'. This had the desired effect and the animal man was ensnared:

> … and [Enkidu] possessed her ripeness.
> She was not bashful as she welcomed
>   his ardour.
> She laid aside her cloth and he rested
>   upon her.
> She treated him, the savage, to a
>   woman's task,
> And his love was drawn into her.

After six days and seven nights of instructive lovemaking, Enkidu became an initiate – possessed of both 'wisdom' and 'broader understanding'. The harlot then led him to the gates of the city, where he took up a new, more civilized, existence – his animal nature having been transformed by his intensely passionate encounter and his new-found knowledge of the arts of love.

♦ ♦ ♦
THE SACRED MARRIAGE
♦ ♦ ♦

The goddess Inanna speaks to her lover:

> *Bridegroom, dear to my heart,*
> *Goodly is your beauty, honeysweet.*
> *Lion, dear to my heart,*
> *Goodly is your beauty, honeysweet.*
> *You have captivated me, let me stand*
>   *tremblingly before you,*
> *Bridegroom, I would be taken by you to*
>   *the bedchamber,*
> *You have captivated me, let me stand*
>   *tremblingly before you,*
> *Lion, I would be taken by you to the*
>   *bedchamber.*
> *Bridegroom, let me caress you,*
> *My precious caress is more savory than*
>   *honey,*
> *In the bedchamber, honey filled,*
> *Let us enjoy your goodly beauty,*
> *Lion, let me caress you.*
> *My precious caress is more savory than*
>   *honey.*[30]

BELOW *Ishtar sits at the window – an image of the goddess as the sacred prostitute.*

The sacred marriage between priestess and king was the most solemn and numinous of all Mesopotamian religious rituals. Through this act, the fecundity and sheer life-force of the goddess was honoured, released, and drawn down to vivify the land and its people. Her blessing was conferred on the earth itself and on the position of the ruling king. Without his wedding to the goddess, in the living form of her priestess, the king was not considered fit or able to rule the people. His temporal potency was inextricably linked with his physical prowess and attuned to his own instinctual sexual energies.

New Year, the 'day of rites', was the time set aside for these ecstatic, hedonistic celebrations. In Mesopotamia, New Year fell at the time of the spring equinox, when the earth was pulsing with fresh, new life. In a feast of collective pleasure lasting many days, the people venerated the divine nature of sexual joy. Everything was designed to stir the senses, and men and women bathed and anointed their oiled skin with herbs and essences. They darkened their eyelids, painted their faces and decorated themselves with jewellery. Scented lotions were used to set curls in their dark hair. Arrayed in all their finery they toasted the goddess and her bridegroom with wine, and performed serpentine, circling dances to the haunting music of lyres, flutes and drums. Sacrifices and libations were made and the perfumed air was thick with the heady scents of cinnamon, aloes and myrrh. In Babylon, a great pyre of incense smouldered atop the legendary, pyramid-like Tower of Babel.

At the peak of this lavish carnival the king approached the temple, bearing offerings of oil, precious spices and tempting foods to lay before Inanna/Ishtar. The crowds thronging the temple precincts chanted sacred erotic poems, creating a highly-charged atmosphere of sensual anticipation and mystical participation. In these poems the goddess, and by extension the priestess who embodied her, prepared for her nuptials with great care:

> *When for the wild bull, for the lord,*
>   *I shall have bathed,*
> *When for the shepherd Dumuzi,*
>   *I shall have bathed,…*
> *When with amber my mouth*
>   *I shall have coated,*
> *When with kohl my eyes*
>   *I shall have painted.* [31]

The sacred marriage took place in the heart of the temple, where the king waited for the goddess/priestess to approach and receive him. One poem describes how the profound religious significance of their union made 'the throne in the great sanctuary' as glorious as the daylight, and transformed the king, who became 'like the Sun-god', literally and symbolically enlightened. Inanna's passion is described in rapturous poetry. The hymns and sacred erotic poems of Mesopotamia celebrate sexuality in a way which reveres its power, inspirational energies and transformative qualities. It is this indivisible fusion of the sexual and the spiritual that formed the core of their religion.

The following sensuous text describes the divine love-making of Inanna and Dumuzi – the consummation of the sacred marriage. It is a continuation of the lines quoted above, and was translated from the Gudea Cylinders (c 3000 BC) from ancient Sumer:

When the lord, lying by holy Inanna,
*　the shepherd Dumuzi,*
With milk and cream the lap shall have
*　smoothed…,*
When on my vulva his hands he shall
*　have laid,*
When like his black boat, he shall
*　have… it,*
When like his narrow boat, he shall
*　have brought life to it,*
When on the bed he shall have
*　caressed me,*
Then I shall caress my lord, a sweet fate
*　I shall decree for him,*
I shall caress Shulgi, the faithful
*　shepherd,*
A sweet fate I shall decree for him,
I shall caress his loins,
The shepherdship of all the lands, I shall
*　decree as his fate.*

LEFT *The biblical Tower of Babel was based on the Babylonian temple of Ishtar.*

Egyptian Sexual Mythology

THE UNION OF CHAOS AND
WIND CREATED MAAT IN HER
FORM AS THE WORLD EGG.

Ancient Egyptian culture is extremely evocative and unique, partially because it seems to have come into being as highly developed in cultural, religious and architectural terms. There is no long evolution towards its final state, but rather a sense that its finest manifestations occurred at the beginning of the civilization, as a theme reflected in Egyptian mythology.

At the core of Egyptian mystical beliefs was the certainty that Egypt had been created by the gods, and life was a gift from those gods. This magical race ruled for almost three millennia and was rooted in a powerful mythology, which it in turn symbolized – the society fed off the myth until it became the myth.

Central to Egyptian religion was the mystery of Osiris and Isis, a powerful mythology which incorporated several myths simultaneously: a fertility myth associated with a society dependent upon agriculture; an astronomical myth which corresponded to the movements of constellations, planets and luminaries; a scientific formula showing principles of nature; a political myth which portrayed the relationship between the two halves of upper and lower Egypt; and an exposition of profound spiritual principles rooted in symbolism. The relationship between Osiris and Isis was also a model for sexuality among the pharaohs, a symbolic manifestation of the fertility myth.

Although so important in Egyptian religion, the Osirian myth existed in many contradictory forms. It has even been suggested that the myth was so familiar to the Egyptians that it was never necessary to state it formally in hieroglyphs.[32] The most common version of the myth is as follows:

Osiris was the son of the sky goddess Nut, and elder brother to Isis, Set, Nephthys and Anubis, and also was the first king of Egypt. His consort was his sister Isis. Together with the god of writing, Thoth, he gave the arts of civilization to humanity. Egypt prospered, but his brother Set was jealous. He murdered Osiris and cut his body into thirteen pieces, which he scattered across Egypt, leaving no heir for the childless Isis. However, she collected the fragments of Osiris and used her magical powers to recreate

ABOVE *Goddess Isis embraces her husband and brother Osiris (Egyptian, Tomb of Seti I). Isis was both sister and husband to Osiris, echoing the Egyptian and gnostic mythology of the goddess being both creator and consort of the god.*

his body, thus making him the first mummy, and had sex with his dismembered phallus (the 13th part) to become pregnant. Osiris was then metamorphosed into the constellation Orion and became ruler of the Kingdom of the Dead and overseer of the rituals of the dying.
Isis hid in the marshes of the Nile and gave birth to a son Horus, whom she raised to become a powerful prince.
Upon becoming a man, Horus fought a duel with Set, during which he lost an eye and Set his testicles.
The outcome of the battle was unclear, but ultimately Horus received the favour of the sun god and ruled Egypt as the first pharaoh and became the eternal eye of Ra.

Each pharaoh in succession was a reincarnation of Horus and his function was to uphold the law, symbolized by the goddess Maat. When a pharaoh died, he joined Osiris in the underworld, while his successor became a new Horus-son and offspring of Osiris and Isis. The myth embodied a duality: the dying pharaoh transformed from Horus to Osiris as the newly crowned heir transformed to the Horus-son of Osiris waiting to become Osiris. The myth was a fertilization myth depicting the birth, death and rebirth of vegetation in nature.

Symbolically, Osiris is the fertilizing effusion of the Nile, the earth is the body of Isis, and Horus is the moisturizing atmosphere. The god Set has a complex symbolism: he is the enemy or protagonist of Osiris, Isis and Horus; the dividing principle of time; the intellect; and also the destroyer. In many myths the generative pair are counterbalanced by the death principle: when the soul incarnates, death is the only possible end result of the process; death, hopefully, leads to rebirth.

What is even more intriguing is that this myth also has direct correlations with Egyptian astronomy. Osiris was associated with the constellation Orion, while Isis was correlated with the fixed star Sirius, the Dog Star in the constellation Canis Major. Because of the latitude of Sirius, its cycle around the earth has the useful characteristic of corresponding

almost exactly to the Julian year of 365.25 days. This meant that its first heliacal rising (when it rose with the sun), which happened in the midsummer zodiacal sign Cancer, was a way for the ancient Egyptians to measure accurately their solar year and integrate it with the more usual, but less exact, lunar year commonly used as a basis for agricultural calendar systems. Sirius (called Sothis by the Egyptians) is the only fixed star which has this characteristic, and the Egyptians took this to mean that it was the higher level centre of our solar system, indeed the 'sun of our sun'. Only in recent years has it been discovered that Sirius could be the star around which our sun orbits within the Milky Way galaxy. If this is true, it is astronomically the sun of our sun because it is the next higher dimension star within our galaxy.

ABOVE *The Papyrus of Ani shows a scene from the Egyptian Book of the Dead, a presentation of the deceased pharaoh by Horus to Osiris, Isis and Nepthys.*

LEFT *The lion goddess Tefnut suckles the infant Horus, watched and protected by Isis and Nepthys. This symbolizes the growth of the sun approaching the summer solstice, which in Egyptian times corresponded to the astrological sign Leo, the lion.*

From the earliest times the movements of Sirius were sacred and the star played an important part in the fertility mysteries of Isis and Osiris, as this passage from the Pyramid Texts shows:

> *Isis comes to thee, O Osiris,*
>   *joyous in thy love,*
> *Your seed rises in her,*
>   *penetrating like Sirius.*
> *The penetrating Horus comes forth*
>   *from thee in his name of*
> *Horus-who-is-in-Sirius.*[33]

Horus was also the sun god, and his rising in conjunction with Isis (Sirius) signalled the unity from which the diversity of the fertile year emerged – an idea central to Egyptian symbolism.

BELOW *Union of sky goddess Nut and earth god Geb (Papyrus of Tameniu, XXI Dynasty, 1040–959 BC). The sky goddess Nut arching over the erect earth god Geb, conceiving the primary quaternity of Egyptian gods, Osiris, Isis, Set and Nephthys. Sexuality was considered to be an integration of heaven and earth.*

♦ ♦ ♦
EGYPTIAN SERPENT GODDESS
♦ ♦ ♦

Serpent goddess symbolism in Egypt is very similar to its Hindu and Buddhist counterparts in that it represents the matrix of the creative male principle. The serpent goddess Mehen enveloped the ram-headed phallic god Auf-Ra every night during his journey through the underworld, a mythic image of the pharaoh's union with the goddess. The goddesses Isis and Nephthys were serpent goddesses because they accompanied souls through the perils of the underworld, and were in turn serpents of the sky. The serpent had a cosmic and

stellar significance in the world above, as well as an underworld symbolism. The goddess's symbol bridges the gap between the two worlds, enhancing her power and mystery.

The Egyptian goddesses and consorts of the pharaoh were often shown with serpent or cobra crowns, and their hieroglyphic names were preceded by the symbol of the cobra, which eventually became the sign for 'goddess'.[34] The pharaoh was identified with the god Ra, who mythically conquered the dragon Apophis, while the enemies he conquered were assumed to be under the influence of a mythical dragon power. Thoth, the god of writing, was also represented as a serpent, signifying his magical wisdom. By these associations, the patriarchal nature of the sacred theocracy in Egypt inherited traces of the cultures of the goddess in earlier times.

♦ ♦ ♦

INTEGRATING COSMIC AND MYTHIC REALITIES

♦ ♦ ♦

The unorthodox but brilliant French Egyptologist Schwaller de Lubicz[35] believed that the sublime purpose of Egyptian religion was to integrate psychologically the two halves of the brain into one, and that their mythology was an encapsulation of basic universal patterns of the natural world.[36] He saw that the function of the hieroglyphs and architecture was to go beyond mental processes or even metaphorical ways of thinking – to transmit deep spiritual ideas in a sensory form so that they could be experienced, rather than merely understood. He attributed the power of Egyptian magic to this phenomenon.

LEFT *Egyptian goddess Isis holding the god Horus (Late Period, c 664–537 BC). The goddess Isis suckles the young solar god Horus, showing that the goddess energy gives birth to the sun and is required to nurture the masculine principle.*

RIGHT *The pharaoh was mystically identified with the god who killed the serpent Apophis, outwardly symbolizing evil, but esoterically being the symbol of generation and the domain of the feminine.*

FAR RIGHT *Egyptian Girl with Snake by Frances Bramley Warren (1889)*

Schwaller de Lubicz's reading of the Osiris myth is that Set represents the Guardian of the Lake of Fire, a mythical location for the battles between Horus and Set, and that he is the principle of the sperm which imprisons spirit in matter.[37] This again refers to the fact that by fertilization we incarnate and become captives of the laws of the physical world until we die. According to the Egyptian Mysteries, cosmic principles called *neters* are primary ideas and formative concepts. Each mystery centre in Egypt expressed an aspect of this knowledge. The creative act of Atum's appearance was revealed at Heliopolis, the work of Ptah was taught at Memphis, the offspring of the genesis was defined at Thebes, and the circumstances of the milieu were described at Hermopolis[38]. Each centre was a whole in itself, yet all centres were required in order to complete the totality.

The Egyptian Mysteries are almost exclusively masculine in conception and manifestation. For example, in the Leyden Papyrus it states: 'All the gods are three: Amon, Ra and Ptah, who have no equals.'[39] They existed before existence, before the sky, before the earth, and before Horus and Set. Each pharaoh is therefore compared to Atum in this genesis of the world, and otherwise treated as the son of Atum. But the Heliopolitan Mysteries put this into perspective by having Atum emerge from the primordial waters (Nun),[40] also before sky and earth were born. Nun therefore is another name for the liquid, primordial feminine matrix, recalling that life originates in the fetal fluids of the womb, and that substance originates as a fire which coagulates into earth, signified by Atum. Atum is both the impulse to life and also the negation of being and origin, a function which, in other cultures, is reserved for the goddess. The resultant black earth is the container, or jailer, of divine light, in that it contains incarnation.

In the Pyramid Texts it is stated that *before* the existence of all things, 'The mother of Pepi who is in the world of the transposed sky, formed him, when this Pepi was put into the world by his father Atum… before death existed'.[41] This implies a feminine form creation from which Pepi arises, but that his father created him. This is consistent with other mythologies where the

RIGHT *Amon drawn through the Realms of Night in his Evening Boat (VIII Dynasty, Thebes). The sun god wears the horns of Khnum as he passes below the horizon and travels in his barque through the underworld every night. Both his departure and arrival the next morning were worshipped by the Egyptians, and considered good times for sexuality.*

BELOW *The lotus symbolizes the unfolding of the spiritual principle from the darkness of the waters in both Egyptian and Indian/Tibetan Symbolism and is also an image of female sublimation in the creation myths.*

female is the form-giver and the male the instigator of the conception.

Further, it is also discovered that Atum was a result of autogenesis, created from the seed of his own loins, that is by masturbation: 'He took his phallus in his grasp that he might create joy in himself, bringing about the twins, Shu and Tefnut.' The seed produced is a model or idea of what it generates – ultimately the seeds of creation are *will* and *thought*. The mysterious boundary between the invisible and the visible is rent, and shows that the essence of both fire and water is required to bring the universe into existence – one cannot exist without the other. In identifying with the myth of the Hindu creation, the masculine principle Atum, by the fire of its heart, projects itself into the feminine watery manifestation of its own self, Nun, in order to bring the world into being.[42]

In the Hermopolitan Mysteries the primordial (feminine) water which appeared with creation already carries the (masculine) hillock of Atum, which in turn makes the water live and breed to produce the sun. From the living water come the serpent neters, grouped as four female and four male principles

LEFT *Forms of the sun god Atum were created by autogenesis (masturbation). Both hold the uas, commonly called the 'key of the Nile', which symbolizes the creative act that divides and generates opposites from the original one.*

BELOW *Osiris, flanked on the left by Hathor and the right by Isis (Old Kingdom Pyramid of Menhaure at Giza). Hathor symbolized female sexuality, inebriation and carnal love as a component of Isis, and is often shown in her triple aspects. She is also the mother, consort and daughter of the sun god Ra.*

with names such as Night, Obscurity, Secret and Eternity. The crawling serpent and frog emerge from the water and form an egg, from which a goose is born. The goose then takes wing and turns into the sun. The mythology of the ithyphallic (erect) snake which creates the world appears once again, in this instance behind the traditional Egyptian creation mythology.

♦ ♦ ♦

THE RECURRING CREATION

♦ ♦ ♦

To the Egyptian, above the real world stood the divine world of male and female deities. The human originates in the divine, but patterns itself after the divine; therefore, the divine world reflects the structures of the human world. Both worlds come into being at the same time and, indeed, interact with each other eternally. The creator gods are paired female and male divinities, which implies that the creator god contains both sets of qualities which separated out into the first beings. In a bizarre twist, the female aspect of the creator god came to be called 'god's hand' – the instrument of masturbation at creation.[43] It is characteristic of Egyptian civilization that although the creator always contains both female and male qualities, he was invariably seen as a male god.

RIGHT *The solar deity Horus with Solar Disk (Egyptian c 590 BC). The god Horus was associated with the reborn sun who passed across the day sky in his barque, bestowing life to all beneath. The Eyes of Horus symbolize the spiritual faculty and the higher qualities of sexuality.*

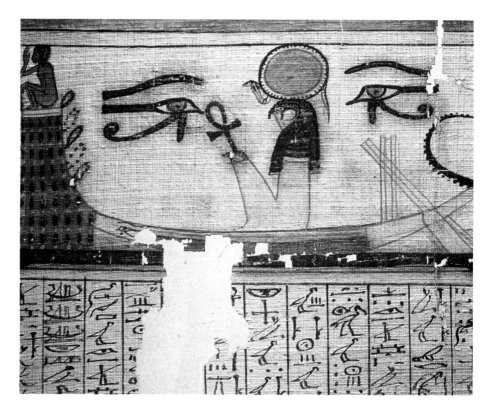

The creation repeats itself every day as the setting sun impregnates the sky goddess Nut and is born again of her the next morning. She is therefore both his consort and mother, while he is both her father and her son, a motif repeated in the attitude to the relationship between a pharaoh, who was both father and son, and his consort, who was seen as both his wife and mother. This loop of generation was characteristic of Egyptian religion.

The many goddesses carried qualities which overlapped so completely that they were seen as aspects of the same great goddess. Thus Isis was the wife and mother of Osiris, while Hathor was the manifestation of female sexuality, inebriation and carnal love. Hathor had a lunar symbolism and her insignia was both the crescent associated with the new moon and the cow horns and sun disk, showing her association with Ra. Hathor also had a dark side as the eye of Ra, where she was a destroyer goddess and identified with the process of rebirth from the afterlife. In this form she often wore a vulture head-dress and the royal serpentine cobra, both identifying her with the divine aspect of the queens and goddesses. Hathor's dual nature, symbolized by the lunar horns, and solar disk, is characteristic of goddess cults originating from the dawn of time.

The uraeus head-dress worn by the goddesses and the pharaoh was a powerful symbol to the Egyptians. The cobra, also revered in Hinduism for its potency and deathly bite, symbolized the duality of life – the active and passive cosmic principles, the movement of the precession of the pole-star through the zodiac,

and the two psychological hemispheres of the brain.[44] Its dual aspect is indicated either by two uraei, or by one uraeus and the head of a vulture, a symbol of manifest femininity. This parallels the symbolism of the *kundalini* serpent of Hinduism, where the energy principle can be utilized in a transcendent way through yogic control, or may be wasted in the satisfaction of desire deriving from lower functions. The uraeus symbol as a crown shows the higher ideal of transcendence which was placed in the capable hands of the king or pharaoh.

◆ ◆ ◆

SISTER MARRIAGE

◆ ◆ ◆

The paradox of the Egyptian succession of pharaohs is that the lines were transmitted through the matriarchal line of the family, from one 'heiress' to the next. Any pharaoh, even though he was the son of a pharaoh, had to legitimize his claim to the throne by marrying an heiress, which meant that he had to marry his sister, or half-sister, as pharaohs often had more than one wife. As studies of the female lines during the dynastic period fail to show that this matriarchal succession was practised, it is assumed that the wife of the pharaoh simply used the title 'king's daughter' whether she was of royal lineage or not.

The theory is that because the gods only married goddesses who were their sisters, the pharaoh, who was in reality a god, could also only marry his sister,

LEFT *Musicians and Dancers Celebrate (Egyptian Tomb of Nebamun, 1400 BC). Magicians and dancers in erotic positions demonstrate the reverence of the Egyptians for sexuality and its component in creativity.*

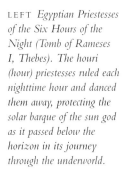

LEFT *Egyptian Priestesses of the Six Hours of the Night (Tomb of Rameses I, Thebes). The houri (hour) priestesses ruled each nighttime hour and danced them away, protecting the solar barque of the sun god as it passed below the horizon in its journey through the underworld.*

ABOVE *The vulture was symbolic to the Egyptians of the divinity that transcended death, and as a symbol it graced the headdresses of goddesses and royal women.*

FAR RIGHT *Egyptian Turin Erotic Papyrus (Pharaonic, XIX Dynasty, c 1295–1186* BC, *Egyptian Museum, Turin) This famous papyrus is unique in depicting prostitutes and their clients in various lovemaking positions. A famous detail is the prostitute painting her lips with a long brush whilst looking into her hand mirror.*

although this practice was limited to the kings. It was known that many pharaohs did marry their sisters or half-sisters, and this fact set them apart and sustained their royal might and importance.[45] There were also father-daughter marriages, such as that of Amenhotep III, whose daughter was called the 'king's wife', but was in fact the daughter of Amenhotep and his principal wife Tiy.

The triad of mother, consort and daughter echoed the triple qualities associated with Hathor and her relationship with the sun god Ra. This is in support of the myth of the birth of the divine king, fathered when Amon-Ra impregnated the king's mother. Since he could not claim this connection until he was enthroned, it was natural that each successive pharaoh was indeed seeded by the sun god. The great paradox is that mothers were often more important than their sons in the matter of succession: they had to have had a relationship with the god to give birth to a son who would become pharaoh, but they could never become pharaoh themselves.

♦ ♦ ♦

THE TURIN SEXUAL MYSTERY CYCLE PAPYRUS

♦ ♦ ♦

The so-called Turin Pornographic Papyrus (Torino 55001) from Deir el-Medina, now in the Egyptian Museum in Turin, Italy, shows a scene of women and men in various situations prior to intercourse. The women seem to be adolescent girls, naked but for their hip girdles and jewellery, and with elaborate hairstyles. The men wear kilts, but grotesquely protruding from them are gigantic male members. Due to the presence of a sistrum and mirror, associated with the goddess Hathor, and the lotus, signifying rebirth, the scene has been taken as an image of fertility, but orthodox sources decline to elucidate or to speculate about what its real purpose might have been. In *Women in Ancient Egypt*[46] Robins has relegated the scene to the last section of the book, where it seems almost to be an afterthought.

One of the manuscripts in the Turin Papyrus shows a series of figures enacting what has come to be called the 'Sexual Mystery Cycle'. Each sign of the zodiac is shown in what is obviously a characteristic sexual position. Although the attribution seems highly doubtful it is none the less very instructive and amusing. All these illustrations make it clear that the Egyptians had a profane and playful view of sexuality, as well as seeing it as a sacred representation of their mystery religion.

There was a similar practice in the Egyptian temples as in the Turin Papyrus of women who were dancing harlots, called *houri*, from the Greek *hora* – meaning hour, because each woman ruled and danced for a certain hour of the night. Their primary religious function was to protect the solar barque of the sun god Ra on its journey through the underworld at night. They kept time throughout the night, just as later Christian monks did with their prayers.[47] Indeed, one of the suggested derivations of the word 'whore' is from the divine houri. In later Persian-Arabian cultures these women were also called houri and were known to dance the planetary hours and guide souls to the stars.

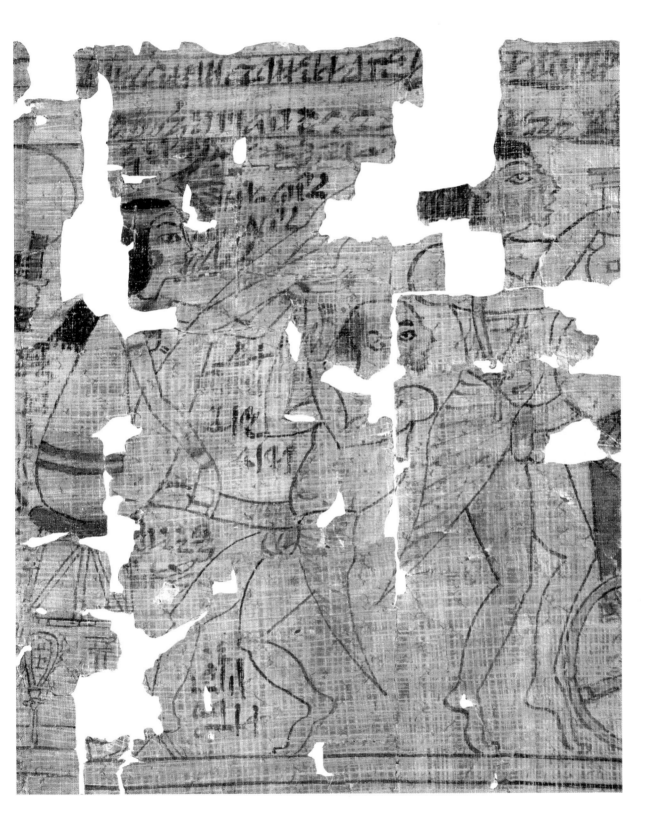

CHAPTER 6

Kundalini Gods and Goddesses

IN THE BEGINNING THERE
WAS NOTHING BUT SELF, IN
THE SHAPE OF A PERSON. BUT
SELF FELT NO DELIGHT IN THE
VOID AND WISHED FOR A
SECOND. SELF THEN FELL INTO
TWO, AND THENCE AROSE
HUSBAND AND WIFE. 'WE TWO
ARE THUS, EACH OF US, LIKE
HALF A SHELL.' HE EMBRACED
HER, AND HUMANITY
WAS BORN.

Upanishads [48]

The fundamental beliefs of Hinduism are transcendent in nature. The manifestation of the gods and goddesses is a primary experience which pervades all life, from womb to grave. According to Indian mythologies, the creator and sustainer of the world, the god Vishnu, periodically descends to earth (incarnates), blessing a womb of flesh with his presence. Each time he descends into the world which he himself made, the forces of evil and destruction are ranged against him. The interplay between opposites therefore always exists and is the way of the world. Indeed, the eternally recurring drama enacted between opposing forces *is* the world.

Vishnu's consort is the goddess Padmā (also called Lotus or Lakshmi) and they are often shown reclining on a bed formed by the coiled cosmic serpent Ananta, who floats upon the waters with his nine heads fanning out to protect them. Lakshmi and Ananta are also aspects of Vishnu himself.

The name Ananta means 'residue' or 'endless', signifying that it is the serpent which remained after the earth was created out of the cosmic ocean.[49] The snake also symbolizes the residue of earlier Earth Mother cults in India, and is also the latent sexual energies contained within the creator god's being. Sometimes the serpent's body is shown running down Vishnu's back, which further reinforces the notion that it is the channel through which the sexual serpent energy rises. The symbolism of the serpent atop the creative cosmic waters of life, enacting the sexual energy which produces life, is common to both Hinduism and Buddhism.

♦♦♦

DREAMING THE UNIVERSE

♦♦♦

As Vishnu sleeps, he dreams the universe. From his navel grows a lotus, as beautiful as his wife with whom it shares its name, and which is the gateway or womb of the universe, the path through which all being comes into manifestation.

The key to the play of opposites is the secret of *māyā*, often seen as the great water or the web of beingness, combining all the processes involved in the generating and taking away of life. The simultaneous interplay of energies that create and dissolve, mirrors the paradox between the dream of Vishnu, which is the world, and the terror of the infinite void of nothingness.

Duality is also manifest in the relationship between *purusha*, the primal male principle, and *prakriti*, the essentially female nature of becoming. Purusha is pure light while prakriti is fertilized by it and births it into manifestation. In the Samkhaya sect, the god Shiva is purusha, and Shakti, which means both 'wife' and 'power', is

RIGHT *Shiva and Parvati (Jain temple sculpture, Khajuraho). Shiva is the creative principle and Shakti allows his physical manifestation in the universe.*

prakriti. The initiating, active male principle is unable to manifest on its own – it is only through the female principle that creation is actualized, bringing reality and generating life.[50] This is represented by images in which Shakti moves while Shiva is acted upon but remains immobile. In such cases Shakti is shown with a halo of flames or fire emanating from her head, while Shiva is pure light. This has obviously sexual references to the distribution of energies during sacred sexuality, and the activity or passivity of the partners determines the roles with which they identity themselves and where their energies are focused.

The distinction between activity and manifestation goes beyond male/female sexuality. The sexual act always requires both activity and passivity. Shiva is unchangeable and spiritual, while Shakti changes, is natural and dynamic, and therefore corresponds to things and beings which exist in the world. Shakti is the active power principle of the male divinity as embodied in his wife, although it is also the female spiritual power made manifest in its own right. This may be part of the reason why the masculine principle is often perceived as being beyond the world, in an ideal reality, while the feminine principle embodies the world and *is* reality.

Just as the Nãga serpent god is shown coiled around the Hindu creator god Vishnu, so he is present where the Buddha is portrayed. As the Buddha sat crosslegged under the Bodhi tree, he became enlightened to the nature of the bondage of all who live and suffer, to the spell which is cast over all who are born to a life which inevitably leads to suffering, sickness, decay and death. After his initial meditation of seven days, he left and sat under a banyan tree for another seven days. Finally, he sat in a state of exaltation under the Tree of the Serpent King.[51] As ferocious thunder threatened, the cobra Muchalinda arose from his hole under the tree and wrapped himself seven times around the blissful Buddha, and with his expanded hood created an umbrella over his head. After seven days the storm passed and the serpent transformed into a beautiful youth.

This legend demonstrates the duality embodied in the serpent, who symbolizes the creative karma of sexuality, birth, death and rebirth, and also points the way to the transcendent realm. The serpent shows the path of the spiralling sexual energy forming an umbrella of transcendence, and yet at the same time it carries the symbolism of the earlier creative functions of the great goddess, united in a higher ecstasy leading to integration. From this symbolism grew the magic of the Buddhist tantras.

Tantrism is a spiritual system, a philosophy, an art form and a way of life which is related to both Hinduism and Buddhism. It acknowledges the existence of both inner and outer realities, and that the primary path to integration is through sexual energy.

Mãyã is identified in tantric teachings with the magical qualities of the female principle of Shakti. It is believed that the manifestation of the world is magical because it has been created by gods, and is therefore illusory and unreal. This is typical of the way in which the female principle is seen as outer reality, and also the principle behind reality. It is obviously there, but also mysterious in its presence.

Similarly, women are loved yet distrusted by some men because they symbolize what is hidden and magical – they carry the onus of everything which is not definite, tangible or real, and yet they are responsible for reality.

✦ ✦ ✦
OUR LADY OF THE UNIVERSE
✦ ✦ ✦

The Hindu conception of the world is described in the Puranas (a collection of the most famous myths describing the deeds of the goddess). The created universe was divided into three worlds (*triloka*) – the earth, the atmosphere and the firmament – when Indra, the king of the gods, slew the limbless dragon, Vritra, in order to release its coils from the cosmic waters. This was the first sacrifice, but it was also the creation of the world, and the 'original sin' of the Indian gods.[52] The Supreme Goddess Devi, often shown as a ferocious tiger or lion, personifies the total energy of creation, and is called the Goddess of the Three Worlds. Indian mythologies portray her as both a benefic creatrix and an implacable ogress who pursues the god-hero Indra for his transgressions.

ABOVE *The Supreme Goddess Maya Devi personifies the total energy of creation.*

LEFT *Vishnu sleeping on the serpent Ananta. (Hindu, 17th century, Rajasthan). The Hindu creator god Vishnu rests between the destruction of the world and the creation of a new universe. He sleeps on the serpent Ananta, who represents eternity, and with Lakshmi, his female consort. At the top left, Vishnu rides Garuda.*

RIGHT *Parvati (Hindu bronze, 13th/14th century). Parvati is the consort of Shiva, and symbolizes spirituality and the power of emerging life.*

The creation of the goddess is an apt metaphor for the coming-into-being of the world. At a time in the distant past, the gods were assailed by a demon-tyrant which threatened to become all powerful. None of the gods could prevail over this great threat alone, so together they channelled their anger and indignation as fire, which issued from the mouths of Vishnu and Shiva, in whom the other gods had taken refuge. Their energies were projected outwards as streams of flames, which then coalesced and grew into the shape of the goddess, complete with eighteen arms.

The gods were so in awe of this perfect manifestation of their energies that they worshipped her as the Primal Female. This was the only way in which their particular and limited energies could be integrated.

As a result of their perfect surrender, the gods had returned their energies to the perfect Shakti, a fountainhead from which they had all emanated in the first place.[53] This renewal was brought about by their return to the initial state of the universe.

When the universe was created by the dismemberment of the dragon, life energy was distributed among many individual manifestations, but this force was lost when they became separated from their source. 'The primal maternal life energy principle reabsorbed them, and took them back into the universal womb. She was now ready to go forth in the fullness of her being.'[54]

This story symbolizes the externalization and projection of our (sexual) energy. The vitality of our body flows out, adopting a bewildering range of wild forms, from the beneficent to the wrathful, according to how we feel.

Our personal universe is composed of such forms, constantly doing battle with each other, fighting for control over the soul of the world, which is also of our making and, in many ways, is us. Our energies transform into other energies, and we can easily become absorbed in their transformations and their illusory existence (*māyā*).

Such absorption can lead us to lose track of the source of our energies. The only path to stillness and peace is through silencing these manifestations and allowing them to return to Shakti, to return into the lotus, and for the lotus to enfold back into the navel of Vishnu. Only in this way can the materialization of Vishnu's dream be reversed.

RIGHT *Buddha on a Lotus Throne beneath the Bo Tree (Burmese, 12th/13th century). The Buddha is seated on a lotus, symbolizing his spiritual unfolding, beneath the Bo Tree and surrounded by scenes from his life.*

♦ ♦ ♦

SEARCHING FOR THE SELF

♦ ♦ ♦

Just as man fully embraced by his beloved wife does not know anything at all, either external or internal, so does purusha, embraced fully by the Spiritual Self, not know anything at all. That is his form, devoid of sorrow, in which all desires are fulfilled; in which his only desire is the Self. [55]

BELOW *Hindu god Indra (Nepalese gilded bronze)*

Rather than investigating and attempting to explain the outer, physical world, as in Western thought and science, Eastern religion and philosophy focus on discovering the core of the inner world, the Self, called in Sanskrit *ãtman*.[56] The Self is changeless, beyond time and space, but lies at the foundation of consciousness and reality. Knowledge of the Self is the primary aim and dynamic activating thought in Indian philosophy. The bliss and profound peace which characterizes experiences of the Self is a counterpole to the changeableness and intangibility, and hence destructive qualities, of life in the world. In this sense, Indian beliefs correspond closely to religious and transcendent ideas of the West, but are very much at odds with the scientific beliefs which form the outer structure of Western thought, although this situation is changing.

Before the Buddha (c 563–483 BC), at a time some hundreds of years before the Greeks were beginning to develop the primary structures of classical Western civilization based on the categorization of knowledge, Indian philosophers were shifting their concentration from the outer world to the inner world by utilizing the psychological, physical and metaphysical techniques of yoga. The first nomadic Aryan herders,[57] to whom the Vedas, Upanishads and Puranas were sacred books, settled vast areas from Greece to India. From many different cultures they collected the earliest religious ritual hymns describing the pantheon of gods, goddesses and other divinities which were the objects of sacrifice and worship. The shift which occurred with Buddhism was to bring within an individual the outer power and magic of the gods and goddesses. The godlike symbols then came to control a person's inner life just as previously they had been seen to create and control the outer world.

Gradually the strict adherence to a life of godly ritual was replaced by the quest for absolute detachment from the outer world of the senses, and the development of ways of understanding the relationship between outer and inner phenomena. In the Upanishads 'being' is metaphorically described as a chariot: the Self, *ātman*, is the owner of the chariot; the body is the chariot, with intuitive discernment and awareness the charioteer; the mind is the bridle; the senses are the horses; and the objects of the senses are the field of the chariot.[58] In an irrational or undeveloped individual, the horses are unmanageable, control is lost and the horses randomly determine the movement and direction of the chariot. An enlightened being, on the other hand, has tamed and yoked his or her mind and the senses are subordinated to higher aims.

Enlightenment means to travel to the supreme abode of the creator god Vishnu, where finally the cycle of rebirth ceases and individuals need no longer spend countless lifetimes being reborn into the world of birth, pain, death, and rebirth. The cycle of birth and death is symbolized by the image of the 'wheel of *samsara*', which depicts the stages of life from birth, through youth, adolescence, maturity, old age and death. On the wheel, along with hunger, sexuality is one of the primary causes of being. All beings are bound to this wheel and inevitably repeat over and over again its basic processes, both the pleasurable ones and, particularly, the unpleasant pain and misery of sickness and death. The goal is to become free of the bondage of the world through the revelation of spirituality.

> *I am neither male nor female, nor am I sexless. I am the Blessed-Peaceful one, who is the only cause of the origin and dissolution of the world.*[59]

The pursuit of freedom from the cycle of rebirth is paradoxically represented by gods and goddesses making love. As the Self lies hidden within all people, so all relationships carry and express the magical goal of integration. The Upanishads say that husbands should not be loved for their own sake, but for the sake of the Self; wives should not be loved for their own sake, but for the sake of the Self; and even children should not be loved for themselves, but for the sake of the Self. The Self is the being, witness, inhabitant and guardian of all beings, and wise ones behold the Self in all aspects of being, not only outside of themselves, but also within.

Pleasure is therefore to be found not in the physical act of sex, but rather in its manifestation of the reintegration of the Self. In a way, sexuality is the Self finding itself in another.

ABOVE *Vajravarahi dakini (Tibetan bronze, 17th century). Female dakini partnering a male Heruka demon are personifications of intense passions, female divinities invoked for granting superhuman powers or Siddhi blessings.*

LEFT *The goddess Durga standing astride the Buffalo Demon, showing the dominance of the sexual Self over its lower nature (13th century Hindu).*

♦ ♦ ♦
KUNDALINI
SERPENT POWER
♦ ♦ ♦

In the ancient yoga[60] tradition the spine is activated by the kundalini serpent in three subtle channels. The spiralling channels through which prāna (subtle life energy) flows are called the *ida* and the *pingalā*, which surround the central channel called the *sushumnā*. Their movement is reflected in the image of the caduceus with intertwining snakes around a winged staff. Kundalini is simultaneously a spiritual force and a sexual force latent within every human, which sleeps at the base of the spine, where it remains as a potent energy. When activated through meditation or aroused by sexual activity, it rises up the spine until it approaches or reaches the crown chakra, at which point the yogi or sexual initiate will experience *samādhi* or bliss. When kundalini is understood and its potency properly channelled, it is a powerful force for spirituality, but

when misused or accidentally activated it can result in permanent psychological and physical damage.

Knowledge of this force is extremely ancient (it was called the 'serpent power', among other names), but it has also been the object of study by psychologists in modern times, most of whom have created their own names for it. Thus Carl Jung compared the kundalini force to his concept of the 'libido'[61] and Wilhelm Reich[62] called it 'orgone energy', which was transmitted by the body but which had its source in the very atmosphere of our planet.

♦ ♦ ♦
ASCENDING THE CHAKRAS
♦ ♦ ♦

The primary belief that the serpent energy (kundalini or prãna) travels up the spine is derived from the philosophy of the chakras ('circle' or 'wheel' in Sanskrit). The many major and minor subtle energy vortexes along the length of the spinal column are connected by channels called *nadis*. Although each chakra is symbolized as a circular wave pattern radiating outwards or as a lotus with a particular number of petals and enclosing Sanskrit meditative syllables, mystic sounds, colours and geometric shapes, this is only the result of visualizations of their powerful but invisible existence. Such imagery is supported by clairvoyants who see the chakras as spheres of radiant energy, revolving at great speed. The medieval mystic Jacob Boehme understood them as being wheels within wheels, all revolving around the spinal column.

The chakras appear as focal points of the union of spirit and matter manifesting as consciousness, paralleling the role

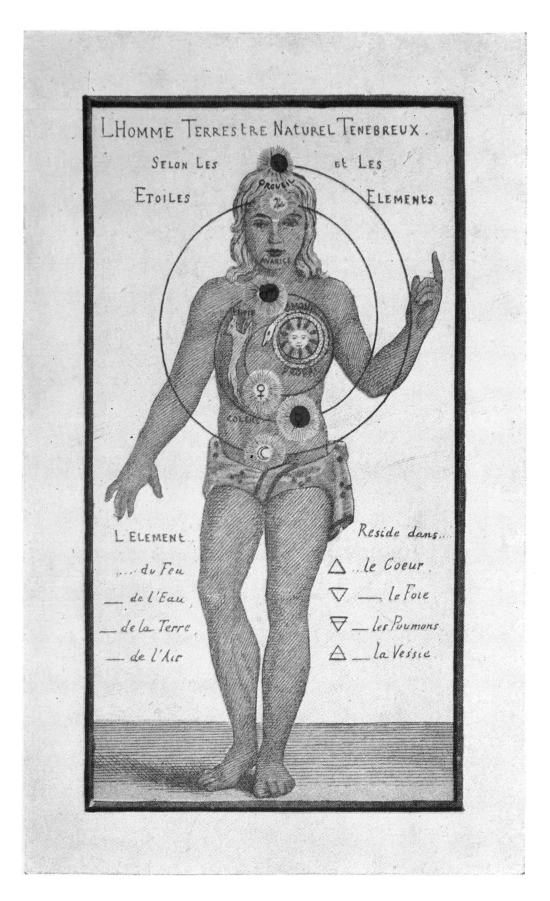

of male and female in many cultures. Indeed Jung considered the chakras 'gateways of consciousness', receiving inflowing energies from the cosmos and spirit. The number of chakras varies according to the many cultures which have utilized this concept. It seems that in original Hindu Tantrism there were believed to be four chakras along the spine, but a later and more common belief is that there are seven. Other Tibetan sources speak of six centres, while in Chinese Taoist alchemical practices there are as many as thirty.[63] It is thought that the seven seals on the Book of Life, mentioned prominently in St John's *Book of Revelation*, are also the chakras, and correspond directly to the seven churches.

The location of the chakras is also variable. The Theosophists placed the chakras on the front of the body. Hindu and Tibetan literature places them along the cerebro-spinal axis. Because they are subtle energies their location cannot be pin-pointed. It is probable that the energies of evolution which are continuously transmitted through all of us activate the chakras in a particular sequence. Involutionary forces pass down from the head to the pubic area, while the evolutionary energies flow upwards through the spine from the sacral chakras to the head. Every individual has a choice about whether to identify with these upward or downward forces.[64] The ascending energies bring the mind into closer contact with the soul and promote integration on a spiritual, sacred level.

Western adherents of the chakra system have correlated the traditional locations with the system of endocrine glands, which closely correspond to the seven spinal chakras.

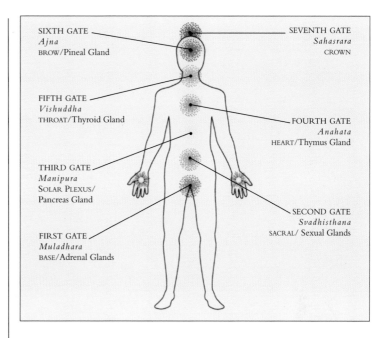

SIXTH GATE
Ajna
BROW/Pineal Gland

SEVENTH GATE
Sahasrara
CROWN

FIFTH GATE
Vishuddha
THROAT/Thyroid Gland

FOURTH GATE
Anahata
HEART/Thymus Gland

THIRD GATE
Manipura
SOLAR PLEXUS/
Pancreas Gland

SECOND GATE
Svadhisthana
SACRAL/ Sexual Glands

FIRST GATE
Muladhara
BASE/Adrenal Glands

In the process of evolving towards higher spiritual states, energies are transferred from lower to higher chakras, which in turn activates them and accentuates their colour in the human aura. It is thought that the Personality, or Lower Self, works through the lower three chakras, while the Spiritual Triad of the higher three chakras (culminating in the Crown chakra) contains energies of all seven within itself. Similarly, Love works through the Heart chakra, Intelligence through the Throat chakra, and Will through the Crown chakra. The path of enlightenment ascends through these states of being, activating the equivalent chakras along the way. The motivating energies are both sexual and psychic in their potential, and it is characteristic that as particular chakras are activated, a corresponding psychic awareness is experienced.

Normally the electric, mystical fire of the kundalini lies coiled around the Base chakra, but when aroused it spirals

ABOVE *The Seven Chakras are gates of subtle energy associated with endocrine glands as they step up the body from the Base to the Crown.*

FAR LEFT *The Seven Chakras (From 'Theosophica Practica'). The seven chakras step up the spine from the Base chakra near the sexual organs to the Crown chakra at the apex of the head. They are spirals of subtle energy which are energized by spiritual and sexual energies and the balancing of these within the psycho-spiritual organism.*

upwards, often burning through the protective etheric webs between the chakras, unless an individual has control over the functions of the Lower Self, signified by the three lower chakras. If this understanding and control have not been established, then he or she is destined to failure, possibly accompanied by psychological and spiritual disturbances which can eventually manifest as physical disease. Indeed, many of the diseases common to modern humanity may originate in the misuse of sexuality in this way. Tantric spiritual exercises are intended to prepare initiates to utilize these precious energies in the proper way. However, even when this lengthy and arduous process is complete it is questionable whether such evolved beings will be able to integrate in our society, such is the prejudice against these practices.

♦ ♦ ♦

MANTRAS, YANTRAS, MUDRAS AND RASAS

♦ ♦ ♦

The earliest tantric practices were derived from Hindu animism and were based on the archetypal male/female relationship cultivated by Shiva and Shakti. Indeed the Shiva cults are very strongly identified with tantra, and their god was shown as hermaphroditic, symbolic of the differentiation of the male and female principles which eternally wish to reunite.

A primary difference between Western love magic and Hindu Tantrism is that in the Eastern forms participants are seen as aspects of gods and goddesses, and their individual personal aspects are virtually eliminated. The ritualistic qualities are exaggerated and the visualization

LEFT *Tantric Initiation (Indian, 18th–19th century) The two principles of the male Shiva and female Shakti (embodying wisdom) merge in the couple and transcend their sexual embrace.*

RIGHT *Vajrasattva in union with Supreme Wisdom (Tibetan bronze, 18th century). This is symbolized by Visvatara. Wisdom is symbolized by the female principle in sexual embrace.*

ABOVE *The 'aum', or 'om' symbol.*

is supported not only by understanding postures and positions, but also by meditating upon tantric symbols which evoke the perfect godly union.

In tantric practice, sexual partners use many devices to encourage identification with Shiva and Shakti. Among these are the desire to transcend physical and sexual limitations, and the assumption of a magical quality to the union. In addition, the process is supported by arcane techniques such as ritual nakedness, *mudras, mantras, yantras* and breathing exercises.

Partners must understand and be initiated into the many magical and ritual positions of lovemaking (mudras), which include hand as well as body positions. These positions are ceremonial and also help create the flow of divine fluids produced by the woman's aroused body, which either open or seal the energetic channels opened in the sexual act.

A primary belief of Tantrism is the correlation of sound with manifestation. It is thought that the universe itself came into being as a primordial sound, the seed-syllable 'AUM' or 'OM' of the god Brahma. The mantras bring partners into the correct mind and vibrational

RIGHT *Erotic Temple Reliefs at Kajuraho (India). These capture the wild abandon and sensuality which Hinduism attributes to the gods and goddesses. The sexual desire which energizes the universe emanates from spirituality, and they are the twin forces of life.*

resonance in which to achieve unity with the creative forces of the universe itself. Mantras are always given by a guru, who chooses them specifically to evoke the correct energies and to encourage the absorbtion of the participants' being in the magical moment. The mantras are sounded as part of breathing exercises, so that the auditory vibrations are correct and support the integration of the tantric experience.

Yantras are the visual equivalent of the mantras – each sound has a geometric pattern of colours and shapes which it brings into manifestation. Each of the seven chakras has a yantra diagram representing its spiritual energies. The position of the lovers' bodies is often similar in form to the yantra diagram which most closely corresponds to the energies they will evoke in the sexual act. During the integration the yantras are visualized, and as the kundalini force rises it activates and literally enlightens each yantra in turn. This continues up to and including the Crown chakra, which resembles a thousand-petalled lotus.[65]

ABOVE *Hindu Sri Yantra Meditation diagram (Hindu, 15th century). The interlocking triangles symbolize the integration of male and female, with the downward-pointing innermost triangle like a vulva showing that this is a goddess yantra.*

The rasas are both the quality of intoxication required for divine transportation and the equivalent emotional states of ecstasy which allow total abandon and encourage the kundalini energies to complete their cosmic circuits.

One of the most powerful characteristics of tantric sexuality is the circulation of the resultant energies. The process is not just about sexual satisfaction for each partner; rather, it aims to circulate kundalini energies between and around their activated and sacred bodies. The entire physiological and psychological systems of both partners are thereby enlivened, reactivated, revitalized and energized. It is a dance in which there is no distinction between sound, psyche, physique and spiritual energy. Hands transmit powerful energies from place to place, and even the feet are important receptors and transmitters of the energy flow. As the energy is initially quite raw, the object of the exercise is to refine it and bring it to a stage where it is pure spirit – literally, a nectar of the gods.

These sexual rituals are understood to operate on three simultaneous levels: the practical or literal level of prescribed body positions, movements and ritual actions; the allegorical level where the body parts, feelings, spiritual mechanisms and additional aids are understood as reflections of godly expressions; and the mystical level where each action is an energetic mechanism which brings the participants closer to final integration with the gods themselves. In a paradox which is no less than the achievement of the unachievable, or an expression of the inexpressible, the participants become other than themselves in order to become more than themselves.

Ideally, the sacred is activated and the profane is eliminated. This releases the participants from the bound quality of living in time and space, and gives them the freedom to transubstantiate their energies and physical movements into higher forms.

ABOVE *Maithuna (Hindu, 11th century)*

FAR LEFT *Thanka of Padmasambhava (Oriental Museum, Durham University). In Tibetan Buddhism it is the function of the enlightened ones to order and centre spiritually and psychically the universe by which they are shown to be surrounded.*

ABOVE *Khajuraho Erotic
Sculptures (Hindu). Erotic
engagements between
gods and goddesses are
characteristic of the love
of Hindus and their
pantheon of deities and
express the sensuality of
life and death.*

♦ ♦ ♦
THE HINDU KAMA SUTRA
♦ ♦ ♦

The standard book of love in Sanskrit
literature, the *Kama Sutra*, was written
by the legendary Hindu sage Vatsyayana,
who lived sometime between 100 and
300 AD. His 1,250 aphorisms on love are
subdivided into smaller verses, parts and
paragraphs and were composed for the
benefit of the world while he led the
life of a religious student at Benares,
wholly engaged in the contemplation of
the deity.

The primary message of the *Kama
Sutra* is that anyone acquainted with the
true principles of sexual science, who
preserves the *Dharma* (virtue or religious
merit), *Artha* (worldly wealth) and *Kama*
(pleasure or sensual gratification), and
who has regard to the customs of the
people, is sure to obtain mastery over the
senses and achieve freedom. By conquering sexuality without becoming a
slave to it, adherents would gain great
material and spiritual success in life. This

is consistent with the sacred function of
sexuality at the highest level of Hindu
society.

The *Kama Sutra* has been the basis of
much Indian religious and sexual art,
sculpture and architecture and has consequently become well known throughout the world. The famous caves at
Ellora and Ajanta outside Bombay are
full of erotic stone carvings illustrating
the integration of male and female principles, as well as showing how the sexual
roles correspond to the being of the god
Shiva and his consort Shakti.

♦ ♦ ♦
MODERN TANTRISM
♦ ♦ ♦

*So saying, the Master Yogi
Lord Shiva takes his
beautiful consort upon his lap,
unites with her and,
rising, they move through
time and space.*[66]

The Hindu and Buddhist view of history
is cyclical. Each world age is graded into
a series of cycles with the earliest cycles
being both the most highly evolved and
the longest. Successive world ages (*yugas*)
decrease in duration and quality, showing
the degeneration of the world from its
initially perfect state. Each cycle begins
and ends with a universal destruction.
From this it can be seen that the initial
knowledge and wisdom of the earliest
stages of humanity's existence have
degenerated from the purity of the first
Golden Age many aeons ago.

We are currently approaching the end
of the fourth and last world era, the Kali
Yuga, the age of dissolution. Therefore
we are counselled that, instead of avoid-
ing the supposed causes of humanity's

downfall – including sex and the use of kundalini energies – by remaining chaste, we should 'ride the tiger' and work with those energies in a constructive way, transforming them into forces for good. It is towards this end that tantric practices were developed in the first place, and they are particularly relevant today. We must take the energy which on the larger scale is causing dissolution (manifested in increased population and violence) and transform it within ourselves. The power of such transformation is a very positive manifestation of tantric practices.

The paradox and rarely understood foundation of tantric sexual practice is that a great degree of inner work is required if the potential danger of sexual energies is to be neutralized and transformed. Therefore much attention is directed to meditation, visualization, a vegetarian diet, physical, emotional and mental exercises and other regimes which focus and direct the individual towards integration. Often this means giving up the very practices or habits most strongly associated with tantra – such as sexual activity – for long periods of time. A primary aspect of many tantric practices is that the aspirant should experience long periods of celibacy and intense purification as a preparation for initiation. In many ways this inner journey is the only possible way to come to terms with the heart of tantric practice.

Tantric philosophy encompasses an enlightened attitude towards sexuality as an essential tool for integration, both within an individual, between couples, and in the universe itself. It is a practical and spiritual path offering deep insights into the powerful dynamics of creativity and the profound integration of relationship. The teachings are timeless, yet merge easily into our present age. Despite the need to be initiated and taught tantric knowledge, once it is acquired it is possible to grow and develop a liberated attitude which is the best possible expression of unity in our world.

BELOW *Paramasukha-Chakrasamvara is a Buddha of the Mother tantra class and he resembles tantric forms of the god Shiva. Here he is depicted with his consort Vajraharahi (Central Asian bronze, 17th century).*

CHAPTER 7

Yin / Yang Sexual Alchemy

ABOVE *Yin / Yang symbol*

The overwhelming influence of Confucius in Chinese culture often presents a puritanical image of their society. One of the most potent symbols of Confucianism is the interplay between the polar, binary qualities of Yang (light, masculine) and Yin (dark, feminine), as expressed in the *I Ching* or *Book of Changes*, and many other aspects of Chinese culture, including medicine, architecture, garden design, painting and philosophy. Since a primary expression of these female and male energies meeting in union is sexual, it is quite natural that there is a valuable tradition of sacred sexuality in Chinese history.

The elaborate and dignified way in which the imperial Chinese emperors reigned – with a profound sense of order, determining the correct relationship of all things, including their own relationships and those of their families – masked a sacred function for sexuality. Under the ordered surface of Chinese history can be seen references to proper conduct with mistresses, who were so well integrated into the civilization that their treatment and the reverence towards them were integral to the success of the society. In other words, the outer society showed a sexual restraint, while the inner society encouraged and even worshipped the function of sexuality as a representation of Yin/Yang integration.

Figurines of naked men and women have been found in tombs, dating back to as early as the Zhou dynasty (approximately 1122–255 BC). The function of these figures was to vitalize the spirits of the dead. The sexual potency of revered ancestors conveyed a profound influence upon their living offspring; indeed, the entire structure of ancestor worship has an underlying sexual connotation as a result.

Chinese porcelain was very influential in encouraging the expression of the sacred function of male and female. Just as the Ming dynasty was the culmination of Chinese art and literature, so too was it the period of the highest expression of erotica. The same connoisseurs who encouraged and delighted in the Ming culture were also responsible for bringing erotica into society. The Imperial Court was a major influence in that it provided a primary market and inspiration for these works of art. Even the materials were of the highest order: silk, paper, porcelain and ivory. Sexual activity was most often presented as peaceful and euphoric and, in fact, was seen as a primary way to create and maintain good health and vitality.

In contrast, early Taoist and Buddhist art created by monastic artisans removed from the affairs of the world, both physically and sociologically, showed sexuality as a characteristic of the hellish states described in the Books of the Dead, where sexual activity was perceived as leading to death. Even within Chinese society there has been a duality about the true role of sexuality.

♦ ♦ ♦

THE TAO OF THE WORLD

♦ ♦ ♦

The Chinese Taoist view of the universe was based upon qualities and mechanisms of chance (and change) in life, which were seen as manifestations of a divine play of opposites. Instead of being ruled by the principle of cause and effect, the Chinese believed there was a correspondence between inner and outer events, a coincidence or synchronicity[67] which binds them together. This binding quality is 'meaning'.

*Dragon Guarding the Yin/Yang Symbol
(Vietnamese, 18/19th century). The dragon,
symbol of imperial power, guards the Yin/Yang
symbol, the pearl of inner energy.*

ABOVE *The Yin/Yang symbol, an integral aspect of the physical world, here shown near a dragon source of sexual energy*

BELOW *Great Yin Talisman (early 12th century) evoking female, dark and earthy energies.*

The terms Yang (light) and Yin (dark) are polar opposite principles in the universe, and all events can be described by their interaction. These polar qualities also correspond to male and female principles. Their interactions are symbolized by a sequence of changes which are regulated by an inexpressible central component, the 'Tao', which is freely translated as the 'Way' or 'Course', but is in itself nothing more than a regulator of the movements. Taoists believed that:

> *The primal powers never come to a standstill; the cycle of becoming continues uninterruptedly. The reason is that between the two primal powers there arises again and again a state of tension, a potential that keeps the powers in motion and causes them to unite, whereby they are constantly regenerated. Tao brings this about without ever becoming manifest.*[68]

The power of the Tao lies in its ability to maintain the world by constantly renewing the tension between the polar opposites. This Tao force surrounds all things, gives them the energy to exist and to complete their functions, and provides an organizing centre for them. This essential quality is an inheritance of all things at creation.

The Tao is magical and mysterious because it symbolizes the series of polar tensions which in many ways *is* the world. Concealed within every individual movement, feeling, sensation, thought or intuition is its integral opposite. The mighty oak tree, for example, manifests its growth when in its prime, but as a seed conceals it, yet they are the same.[69] The Tao hides its power by moving from within outwards in manifestation and, simultaneously, from without inwards in regeneration. These phases are continually reversing themselves. For this reason the Tao is impossible to locate.

As the *Tao Te Ching* says,

> *The Tao that can be expressed is not the eternal Tao.*[70]

Opposites tension each other but also complement and complete each other. Their dance is a constantly moving process which aims to attain balance through change. Flowing with change is life. Resistance to change on the other hand is death.

The Tao reveals itself differently to every individual, according to his or her nature. It is said that the wise discover its workings behind all things, while all others see only what meets their eyes.

♦♦♦
CULTIVATING LIFE ENERGY
♦♦♦

The hidden, formless and silent source which animates the Tao is a dynamic energy called *ch'i* equivalent to the Hindu yoga term *prāna*. Although to Western minds ch'i would be a type of bio-energy, the Taoist ch'i is equivalent to what is known as the soul, and is an air or breath energy considered to be feminine and receptive in its action. Its polar opposite is the spiritual *ching* sexual essence residing within the male sperm. In one or another of its forms, ch'i is considered to be the primary energy upon which we draw throughout our lives. It originates in the burst of energy released during the sexual act of our own conception, and dissipates continually throughout our lives. Similarly, there is a universal form of Ch'i (with a capital C), which is the total energy generated by the creation of the universe, and which diminishes through the process scientists have identified as entropy. There is obviously a resonance between cosmic and individual ch'i.

In the Chinese art of harmonizing the landscape, called *feng shui* (literally wind and water), the serpent is seen as symbolizing the flow of mysterious earth energies, breaking the surface with its back and creating rows of mountains and the twisting rivers of the landscape as a result of its undulations. The extent to which the ch'i energies of the earth animate the landscape dragon varies according to the time of day or night, the ebbing or flowing of tides, and the time of the year. The blood of the dragon is thought to transmit the life energy which sustains all living creatures, and humanity is especially reliant upon and sensitive to its force. The dragon's cave is found at particularly auspicious sites where earth energies converge and natural conditions support the accumulation of its energy. These magical places are sought out by practitioners of feng shui.

According to Chinese medical lore, the running-down of ch'i may be the most important factor in determining the length of human life. Many factors drain a person of ch'i, including poor diet, improper breathing, environmental pollution, consumption of alcohol, tobacco and drugs, but the improper use of the sexual orgasm is one of the foremost, particularly for men. Ch'i may be improved by dietary means, breathing exercises, herbs and other Taoist

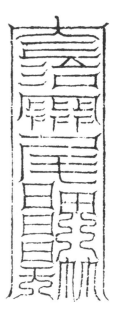

ABOVE *Great Yang Talisman (early 12th century) evoking male, light and heavenly energies.*

BELOW *Painting of woman on a balcony (China, 18th–19th century).*

ABOVE *Chinese dragons painted on a wall in Haw Par Villa, Singapore.*

RIGHT *Head of a dragon on a pot which stands in the Mandarin hotel, Beijing, China. It forms part of the feng shui energy flow.*

ABOVE *Golden dragon on a door at Haw Par Villa, Singapore. Dragons were viewed as beneficent powers.*

techniques, but the correct use and regulation of sexual energies is particularly effective. Indeed, the conservation and replenishment of ch'i is a central concept of Eastern medicine in all of its forms. Eastern philosophy contains an exact science of life energy, and disease is seen as a degeneration of the pure and potent energy received at conception. It is when there are energy imbalances that symptoms of disease manifest themselves in the corporeal body.

In a life of wisdom a central goal is to integrate vital energies and enact a transformation which will unify soul and spirit in order to create a higher, immortal body – symbolized by the Chinese as the 'Golden Flower'. The Chinese are 'holistic' in their views because they understand that sexuality is not just a component of overall balance without and within, but is a central mechanism for either getting into or out of balance.

ENERGY MOVEMENT AND MERIDIANS

♦ ♦ ♦

The Chinese believe that life energy travels throughout the body along a network of invisible channels called meridians. Each of the 12 major meridians is associated with a particular organ, endocrine gland or other vital function, and is complemented by many minor meridians. The objective of healing techniques such as acupuncture is to activate meridians which have become blocked and restore healthy energy flow to organs and vital functions. Similarly, it is believed that the correct use of sexual energies has a curative effect and stimulates and cleanses the meridians, while their misuse will contaminate them.

The connection between the healing process and sexuality is natural and important. Chinese philosophy claims that we are composed of more than two distinct levels of being called body and spirit. Instead, there are three contiguous aspects of being which interrelate with each other: the 'body', a stem connecting the energetic ch'i 'roots' with the flowering 'spirit'. The process of integration operates in many areas of life, such as diet, breathing, meditation, right behaviour, exercise and sexuality. The ultimate goal is twofold: first, to return the body to its primal energy and potency, and second, to transform the living body into a higher, spiritualized entity which transcends life, a state referred to as the 'Golden Flower' or the 'Union of the Triple Equation', both of which correspond to the integration of heaven and earth.

ABOVE *Talisman of the Heavenly Yang is a cure for women. It symbolizes a penis carrying the characters 'induced to come' under a stellar constellation. The illness caused by imbalance of Yin and Yang is corrected through sexual intercourse.*

♦ ♦ ♦
TAOIST SEXUAL ALCHEMY
♦ ♦ ♦

The principles guiding Chinese sexual practices were applied in the higher levels of Taoist society by sages and their emperors. Certainly this was something that few ordinary people practised or even knew about, but was rather a secret path reserved only for initiates and their concubines.

One of the primary ideas of Taoist philosophy and sexuality is that the human sperm carries a powerful life energy in addition to its fertilizing potency. It is therefore to be understood and treated as a treasure to be guarded, rather than as a resource to be squandered. Male ejaculation for purposes other than producing children was considered to be the ultimate folly, and when it occurred over extended periods of time was believed to have had a profoundly negative effect on the health and well-being of a man. While today this may sound far-fetched, consider that a single ejaculation contains between 200 and 500 million sperm cells, roughly equivalent to the population of the United States, and takes up to a third of a man's daily ration of energy.[71]

Even one ejaculation constitutes a great strain on a man's energy system and his general state of health, particularly as it reduces the efficiency of the glands which constitute the immune system. This degeneration and its attendant weaknesses can have several effects: it can lessen future potency, make any kind of energetic transformation difficult if not impossible, and may produce an unconscious anger towards women.[72] It is paradoxical that a sensation which brings such ecstatic pleasure is in reality a harbinger of great energetic difficulties in later life. Ejaculation is a momentary, superficial pleasure when compared with the deeper, more profound experience possible when the seed is not lost but recirculated within the body, and even more so when the sexual energies are circulated between partners.

Taoism is unique in not being against sexuality in principle, as is the case in many other world religions, which attempt to control this vital and important energy source. Taoists have never promoted celibacy as a solution for the potential misuse of sexual energies; rather, they have evolved sophisticated ways to heighten the sexual experience and at the same time create a profound spiritual objective for the process.

The primary principle of Taoist sexuality is the cultivation of the seed through retention. The techniques are many, but the primary mechanism is the sealing of the penis through exercises for increasing pelvic strength, practised first without contact with the opposite sex. Either by utilizing the scrotum as a diaphragm to pump sperm upwards (with a sacral or cranial pumping action) or by using a testicle breathing method and other auxiliary support techniques such as meditation and breathing, a man may 'lock the gate' or create a 'power lock'. This action not only sends the ch'i upwards into higher centres of the body, but also generates profound healing effects. Among these effects are a primary detoxification of the body through increasingly effective bowel movements, a modification of the saliva, elimination of haemorrhoids, and a purification of the blood.

When the power lock is understood and the body and mind trained for a period of time, ranging from weeks to months or years, it may be applied to higher meditative practices as well as the actual sexual act. The first stage of the process involves the ability to focus the ch'i energy in the navel region and to store it for use in prescribed ways. The spiralling, swirling energies thus generated are transformed into states of higher fusion as they climb upwards towards the crown of the head. The power lock prevents the essential seed from escaping, while more developed exercises direct it to higher tasks.

ABOVE *Acupuncture meridians on a Yin/Yang symbol*

RIGHT *Acupuncturist's chart showing the meridians, channels through which the ch'i energy is thought to flow around the body.*

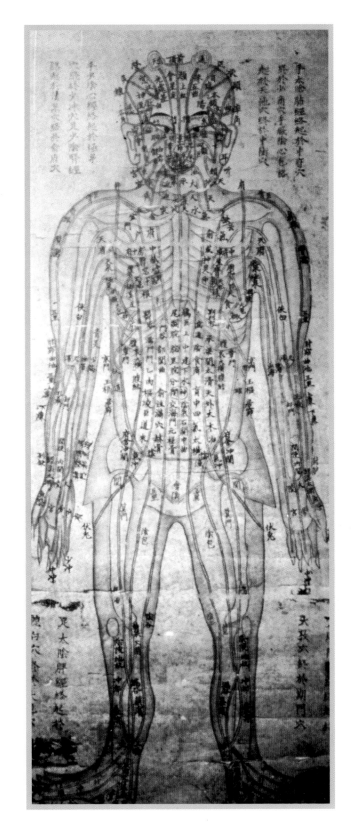

RIGHT *A soldier embraces his lover.*

One effect of such ejaculation control is to send sexual energy upwards through the body towards the head, activating the acupuncture meridians and the chakras along the way. These Taoist practices are considered a form of alchemy as they have the ability to transform lower energies into higher ones. Ultimately, this energy is sensed in the mouth, where it creates a fantastic taste like that of honey nectar. This higher product of Taoist alchemy is alluded to as a life elixir with miraculous powers of regeneration, sustaining sexuality for decades and producing extreme longevity in practitioners. The substance is ethereal, but many references to it exist, often poetic: the 'Seed Pearl' or the 'Secret of the Golden Flower', or the 'amrita' or elixir of life in the Hindu yogic culture, or the 'nectar of immortality'.

♦ ♦ ♦

TAOISM AND WOMEN

♦ ♦ ♦

The Taoists are quite open about their views on the role and position of women, giving them great power but not much acknowledgement. While during certain eras of Taoism it was understood that frequent sexual contact with the same partner, regardless of the quality of that contact, was of less value to both partners than having sexual relations with multiple partners, it is generally accepted that the truest Way (the Tao is also called the 'Way') is monogamous. The *I Ching* recounts how it was common for noble, wealthy or powerful men to have households with many women, complete with mistresses and secondary wives in addition to a primary wife. It was believed that sexual activity between the master and all his women

ensured harmony at home and that the potency of a man required that he service all the women in his household. As a primary reason for this contact was to administer Yang energy to the women and, conversely, for the master to obtain sufficient Yin energy from his women, it was justified in the higher levels of Taoist society.[73]

A Taoist sage is aware of the various sexual parts of a woman's body and the secretions which are available to be tasted during the sexual act. The tongue and lips, breasts, and the Mound of Venus are referred to as the 'Three Peaks', which are to be licked, caressed and sucked in order to stimulate a woman and give her maximal pleasure, as well as giving the male healthy substances which will benefit him in ways beyond description. Thus

ABOVE *The Taoist goddess of mercy, Kuan-Yin (China, 17–18th century)*

BELOW *Taoist Sages admire the Yin/Yang symbol (China, 17–18th century). The Yin/Yang symbol is central to Taoist philosophy.*

三第

ABOVE *One of the eight
Pure Ones shown as a
Taoist priest presenting a
phallic (yang) audience
tablet at a celestial altar.*

ejaculation. 'Clouds and rain' is a common expression for lovemaking, and its variants describe the entire range of possible sexual situations where, for example the 'rain passes over' or the 'clouds are filled to bursting'.

Just as a lack of ejaculation control is the primary reason for energy loss in men, so menstruation is the primary avenue for energy loss in women, according to the Taoists. Just as male sperm can be rerouted onto an energetic inward path, so can the energy contained within the perfect ovum produced in a woman's monthly cycle be transformed and utilized in the service of higher energetic and spiritual functions. The ovum contains ching energy which is fed by food, breathing and life energy, but also carries potent healing energy which restores the operation and function of other organs. The forces feeding off and squandering this energy in undeveloped women give rise to stress caused by negative emotional states. The positive force for transformation is thus lost and the hormonal centres and organs are deprived of their primary source of natural healing energy.

The task for women is to maximize this sexuality and use exercises to transform potentially negative emotions into positive ch'i energies, which they can then use to integrate with their partners, pass on to their children through creative conception, and use to restore and revitalize their own physical and spiritual systems. Again, it is necessary to learn the various techniques which recycle the ch'i energy around the body and pass it from partner to partner in order to heighten the sexual ecstatic experience, increase the ch'i energy and transform it to higher levels.

the twin peaks of her breasts create an essential 'White Snow' which is sweet tasting, the 'Dark Gate' which protects and is almost always closed, guards the Mound of Venus, and 'Moon Flower' essence emanates from the 'Palace of Yin' located there. The highest peak is the 'Red Lotus Peak', from which the 'Jade Spring' flows through ducts under the tongue.[74] This example of the poetic and inspired worship of the female body and the sexual act is characteristic of Taoist adepts. The names are evocative of the elemental gatherings, higher principles and exalted feelings which their writings and paintings inspire. Clouds symbolize the increasingly powerful female sexual essence activated through intercourse, while rain is male

ABOVE *Demonic couple from the Char Narayan in Patan, Nepal. The demonic qualities associated with sexuality may arise from the lack of control of the partners.*

ABOVE *The 'Great Ultimate', Tai Chi, expressed in sexual terms as the magic union of Yin and Yang. The lovers are in the Taoist 'Hovering Butterflies' posture (porcelain, mid-18th century, Ch'ing dynasty).*

The processes for transformation of the female sexual system are similar in principle to those used by men.[75] One method involves using the breath to revitalize the ovaries, another is to practise and utilize Ovarian Draw to gain, increase, collect and transform valuable ovarian energy instead of releasing it through clitoral or vaginal orgasms. Orgasm still occurs but functions as a revitalizing process rather than a release valve for the negative emotions accumulated during day-to-day life.

When these processes are practised regularly they lead to improved sexuality, promote closer relationships between women and men, and have beneficial healing effects upon skin, bodily organs and sexual organs. Various difficulties associated with menstruation and menopause can also be relieved by the expert use of these practices. Indeed, it is believed that Buddhist nuns had perfected techniques which enabled them to eliminate their menstrual cycles altogether. This was known as 'Slaying the Red Dragon'.[76]

◆ ◆ ◆
THE INTEGRATION OF WATER AND FIRE
◆ ◆ ◆

It is obvious when reading about Taoist sexuality that there is an exaggerated bias towards men and their ejaculative functions. This may be because it is men who are most in need of a higher understanding of the deeper and inner meaning of sexuality. Certainly, the Yang essence of women is recognized as being more powerful than the Yin essence of men, both spiritually and sexually. Men are deemed to be more vulnerable and weaker in their being and in their deeper instincts, hence the profound over-compensation for this fact in patriarchal societies.

The key to sexual harmony is in the rhythmic integration of Yin and Yang principles, which produces a flow of energy from partner to partner, and a circulation from being to being. At a deep level, Taoist sexual philosophy parallels the Taoist view of the world. Integration begins with the circulation of energies within an individual, and this principle can be extended to include a partner of opposite polarity. This is then a process which embraces and reflects the mechanism of the world itself and can be extended outwards into the world, projected through behaviour. It is important to understand this intrinsic principle because it is also, by extension, an underlying principle which modern humanity has 'discovered' in ecology – that of coexistence with the environment through equality of exchange rather than exploitation and rape.

The primary function of much of Taoist philosophy is to promote healthy relationships between people. The lessons of Taoism can be applied to all types of relationships, not only those between male and female in heterosexual marriage. They stress discrimination, an understanding of energy flow to ensure mutual sensitivity, control over blind and animalistic passion, and a focus on mutual enlightenment.

In order for a truly human ecology to function, it is first necessary to understand that no one party can have all the energy. Should this happen, whoever the party, there is stagnation and death. The energetic process can only function perfectly if the energies are circulated and never stop. The movement from breath to sexuality to spirit is a sequence which circles around like the Yin/Yang symbol which is characteristic of such a flow. It is a never-ending cycle which *is* life.

Taoists liken the male/female integration of Yin and Yang energies to a metamorphosis of body and soul. This again is a reflection of the meeting of earth and heaven, the primary principle of Earth Mother cults thousands of years ago. While the outer form of this integration is the sexual act, there are both inner and higher aspects of the process. Within the bodies of the participants the subtle seed fertilizes the higher ovum, and the essence of their souls is purified and transformed. The differentiated masculine being must be continually exposed and influenced by the receptive embrace of the female soul, which it must then distil.[77] The integration creates the 'Golden Flower', a psychological and spiritual centre within which is experienced as a profound light source.

Jung identified a psychological process in some of his patients which was analogous to the creation of the 'Golden Flower'. He described people who were psychically broken apart by the strength

of the polarities of male *(animus)* and female *(anima)* energies within them. This state continued until the integration of the energies took place, resulting in some sort of androgynous unity. In cases when such an integration is necessary, it is likely that sexuality is more of an inhibition than a positive growth factor, but in general the path of Taoist sexual alchemy is one where sexuality is understood as a catalyst for higher integration.

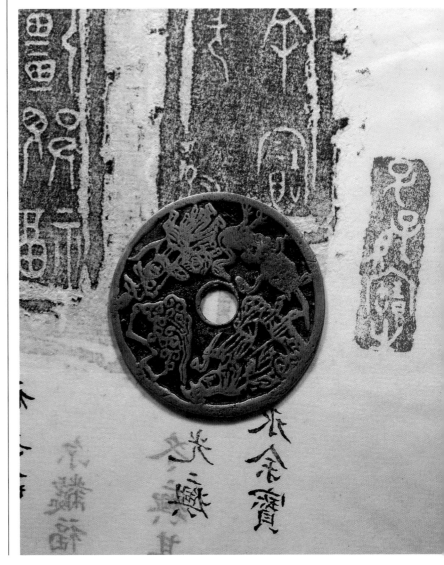

BELOW *Pictographic writing from bronze urns, produced around the time that Lao-Tzu, the master of Taoist literature, was flourishing. The medal shows the four directions of Chinese cosmology, rooted in the dualism of Yin and Yang.*

CHAPTER 8
Greek Goddesses Underground

FAR RIGHT
Venus-Aphrodite with one of her mythic consorts, the beautiful Adonis, painted by Cornelisz van Haarlem (1562–1638)

HYMN TO THE GREAT MOTHER

Gaia, mother of all
foundation of all
the oldest one.

I shall sing to Earth
She feeds everything
That is in the world.

Whoever you are
whether you live upon her sacred ground or
whether you live along the paths of the sea
you that fly

It is she who nourishes you
from her treasure-store,
Queen of Earth
through you

beautiful children,
beautiful harvests
come

The giving of life
and the taking of life
both are yours

Happy is the man you honour
the one who has this
has everything.[78]

Of all the mythic pantheons of gods and goddesses, the Olympian Greek model is arguably the most familiar to us today. The planets in our solar system are named after the Roman versions of these immortal beings, and we still use words which recall their Latin and Greek names – 'aphrodisiac', 'mercurial' and 'jovial' are just three examples.

GREEK/*ROMAN* *Gods and Goddesses*
ZEUS/*JUPITER* *Father figure, with dominion over the skies*
HERA/*JUNO* *Wife of Zeus/Jupiter, patroness of marriage*
APHRODITE/*VENUS* *Goddess of erotic love, beauty, arts*
ARES/*MARS* *God of war, lover of Aphrodite/Venus*
DEMETER/*CERES* *Goddess of fertility and agriculture, especially corn*
PERSEPHONE/*PROSERPINA* *Maiden goddess, daughter of Demeter, Queen of the underworld*
PLUTO/*HADES* *God of the underworld, brother of Zeus, abductor and husband of Persephone/ Proserpina*
ARTEMIS/*DIANA* *Virgin huntress, Lady of the Animals, patroness of virgins*
ATHENA/*MINERVA* *Goddess of war and wisdon, patroness of the city of Athens in her Greek form, born from the head of Zeus*
HESTIA/*VESTA* *Goddess of the hearth, the heart of the home*
POSEIDON/*NEPTUNE* *God of the oceans, brother of Zeus*
HERMES/MERCURY *God of travellers, language, and tricksters – the messenger of the gods*

Yet the Greek pantheon is laid upon the fragments of the cults of the Great Goddesses Inanna, Ishtar, Isis and the all-powerful Minoan goddess of the double axe. Successive waves of Indo-European invaders gradually destroyed the mysterious Minoan and Mycenaean culture of Crete, and that of mainland Greece. The old sacred marriage rituals of the goddess were gradually subsumed, while the goddess herself was divided into a number of figures, each with her own sphere of influence. Zeus, the sky father, whose weapons were the lightning bolt and the thunderclap, became acknowledged as all-powerful leader of the gods. However, despite later myths which gave Zeus the power of 'motherhood' – Athena, goddess of wisdom, sprang from his forehead, while Dionysus, anarchic god of ecstasy, grew to maturity sewn up in his thigh – the goddesses remained powerful and still symbolized fertility, sexuality, birth and death. It should not be forgotten that Zeus's symbols of masculinity, the lightning bolt and thunder, were precious gifts from his grandmother, the original creatrix and Earth Mother, Gaia.

♦ ♦ ♦

MAIDEN, MOTHER, LOVER

♦ ♦ ♦

*The great and amorous sky
    curved over the earth,
and lay upon her as a pure lover.
The rain, the humid flux
    descending from heaven
for both human and animal,
    for both thick and strong,
germinated the wheat,
    swelled the furrows with fecund mud
and brought forth the buds
    in the orchards.
And it is I who empowered these moist
    espousals,
I, the great Aphrodite.*[79]

Golden Aphrodite, goddess of erotic love, of beauty, art and harmony, was born from the white foam of the sea, fertilized by the severed genitals of the sky god Ouranos, Gaia's consort. Her traditional place of birth, Cyprus, hints at her ancient lineage, for she came there from Mesopotamia, carrying with her many aspects of the ancient great goddesses.

LEFT *Aphrodite, refined patroness of sexual love, is seen with Pan, who personifies lust and the spirit of nature.*

RIGHT *An ancient Greek prostitute feasting (c 510 BC)*

Later Greek myth tried to tame her capricious nature by 'marrying' her to crippled Hephaestos, the dour iron-worker, smith, and archetypal jealous husband. Inevitably, such a bond could not contain her, and she betrayed him with Ares, god of war. Hephaestos ensnared the lovers in a golden net he had made, and exposed them to the ridicule of the gods. But Aphrodite simply fled to her birthplace and, as the joyful personification of sexual love and creativity, refused to be diminished in either myth or the hearts of the men and women who paid her tribute.

♦ ♦ ♦

EROS AND ADONIS

♦ ♦ ♦

Aphrodite's other mythic partners reflect her origins more clearly. She is inexorably linked with two: Eros, who hatched from a silver cosmic egg that grew in the womb of night, and her equal before he became known as her son; and the supremely beautiful Adonis, born from a myrrh tree and hidden by Aphrodite and Persephone in the underworld.

Eros's traditional role is to bewitch human hearts, to cause them to fall in love. Like Aphrodite, he personifies the uncontrollable nature of love and sexual attraction and suggests links with fate for, like Aphrodite herself, he is an irresistible agent of destiny. The compelling nature of erotic love was therefore still being honoured as a divine force, but had already begun to lose sight of its connections with transformation and transcendence.

RIGHT *The Horae, mythic dancers associated with Aphrodite as goddess of time and fate*

Adonis (meaning 'Lord') is, like Eros, sometimes called Aphrodite's son, although she never gave birth to him. However, she fought for him with the Queen of the Underworld, Persephone, who had guarded and hidden him, as an infant, from jealous eyes in her shadowy kingdom.

When the dispute was resolved by Zeus, Adonis was allowed to spend part of the year with Aphrodite as her consort, but was symbolically sacrificed annually upon his return from the underworld. In Alexandria, Greece and Syria, his role as Aphrodite's lover and his death and resurrection were celebrated with great public rituals. These variously celebrated the couple's sacred marriage and mourned the inevitable demise of the son/lover as his effigy was cast upon the waves or into the river. His symbolic rebirth was commonly celebrated the following day, echoing erotic fertility rituals all over the ancient world.

OVERLEAF *Dionysus reclining with his entourage*

BELOW *Eros, carved on a tomb, reveals the timeless links between ecstasy and death.*

♦ ♦ ♦
SACRED PROSTITUTES
♦ ♦ ♦

Aphrodite, like the Babylonian and Sumerian goddesses before her, was also celebrated by the widespread ritual of sacred prostitution, most famously in Cyprus, her birthplace, and at Corinth, one of the wealthiest cities in the ancient world. Sacred prostitution no longer exists and is a difficult concept for the modern mind to grasp. Today prostitution is widely regarded as a vice which degrades and diminishes all those involved. However, thousands of years ago the sexual and the spiritual were not so neatly divided. The priestesses of Ishtar in Sumeria became sacred prostitutes in honour of their goddess and bore no stigma – indeed the reverse was the case. For example, a Sumerian clay tablet text places these words in the mouth of the goddess Ishtar, 'A Prostitute compassionate am I.'

Aphrodite's worshippers simply continued this ancient tradition which honoured erotic love as a symbolic and actual sacrament. Amongst her many titles, the goddess was known as 'Aphrodite the Courtesan', 'Aphrodite Who Writhes', 'Aphrodite of the Night', and the 'Heavenly Mother of Loves'. At Corinth, Cyprus and Mt Eryx in Sicily, her sumptuous and thriving temples must have been an astonishing sight, for each was served by more than one thousand sacred whores, *hieroduli*, or *Horae*.

Hesiod, a Greek poet from the 8th century BC, observed that these priestesses of the goddess 'mellowed the behaviour of men', for they not only cultivated the arts of love, but were renowned for their healing powers and learning. The Horae, like all sacred

prostitutes, were also graceful dancers – the Dance of the Hours derived from their custom of marking the hours of the night with circling dances. This rite reflects Aphrodite's role as goddess of time and fate, as well as her patronage of arts, music and culture.

As Greek society became increasingly patriarchal, the temple harlots lost the power and status of the Sumerian priestesses. Many of them belonged to the slave class, for wealthy men would buy women at the slave markets and make a gift of them to Aphrodite's temple. As the handmaidens of Aphrodite, they burned the 'golden tears' of fresh frankincense, celebrated their goddess, and were still revered as her embodiment here on earth. However, their sexual rituals were but a faint echo of the elaborate, sacred, ritual marriage of the Sumerian king and temple priestess, in which they sought the blessing of the goddess Ishtar on all their endeavours, and without which the king could not rule effectively in the eyes of his people.

ABOVE *Hades banqueting in his underworld kingdom*

FAR LEFT *Demeter with her consort Triptolemus and her maiden daughter, Kore, also known as Persephone*

♦ ♦ ♦

DEMETER AND THE
MYSTERIES

♦ ♦ ♦

The ritual of sacred marriage also sur-vived at the secret heart of the Mysteries at Eleusis. These rites were held in honour of another golden goddess, Demeter, who represented the fecundity of the body and the cultivation of the earth itself. Her enduring symbol is a sheaf of ripe corn. Her daughter, the maiden Persephone, is central to her myth and to the Mysteries themselves, which re-enacted the maiden's loss and eventual restoration to her sorrowful mother. Persephone, innocently picking flowers in a sunlit meadow, was brutally snatched away by the dark god of the underworld, Hades, to become his unwilling bride. Demeter's outraged grief brought barrenness to the earth as she wandered in search of her beloved daughter. Her meandering brought her to Eleusis where, disguised as an old crone, she initiated the king into her mysteries and revealed to the people the secrets of agriculture. In the myth, a deal is eventually struck with Zeus, and Persephone is allowed to spend two-thirds of the year above the ground with her mother, returning to her grim hus-band during the winter months only because she ate some of the pomegran-ate which Hades offered her while she was in his domain. The pomegranate symbolizes Hades' seed, or sperm. The seed is bitter, as befits the Lord of the Underworld, but it is enclosed in sweet red flesh which symbolizes his passionate nature. By eating the fruit, Persephone received his male energies – of her own free will. Having symbolically accepted him, she must become his bride. This

LEFT *Dionysus's Eastern origins are suggested by his appearance with leopards. Here he rides the animal (c 180 AD).*

RIGHT *Demeter presides over an initiation rite in the Eleusian Mysteries.*

story predates the biblical tale of Eve eating of 'the fruit of the Tree of Knowledge of Good and Evil'. Persephone, in eating Hades' fruit, has knowledge of him – an old way of describing sexual intercourse.

Persephone's underworld marriage is balanced in early tales by the sacred union of her mother, Demeter, with a lover who goes by a number of titles. In Hesiod's *Theogony* (around 700 BC), he is named as Iasion the Cretan hero. Demeter and Iasion make love in a ploughed field, both to ensure the fertility of the earth and as a symbol of Demeter's rulership of the agricultural arts. Ploughing is also a timeless symbol for making love, as revealed in sacred Sumerian erotic poetry.

Demeter is additionally linked to Dionysus, a god whose lineage stretches all the way to India, where he is undoubtedly connected with tantric mysteries. At Eleusis, known to the ancients as 'The place of happy arrival', Dionysus appears as a new-born child, further amplifying the message of death and rebirth which seems to have been the principal theme of the celebrations and secret ceremonies.

The Mysteries at Eleusis remain tantalizing, elusive, and essentially mysterious; although there is a myriad of hints and allusions to them in many ancient texts. Certainly, they involved initiation ceremonies undertaken in darkness, ritual sacrifice, and an assurance that the dead are resurrected and restored to life – just as the earth begins to teem with life in the spring.

A sacred marriage between the life-giving rain and the earth from which all life springs represented the culmination of these solemn rites. The Bishop of

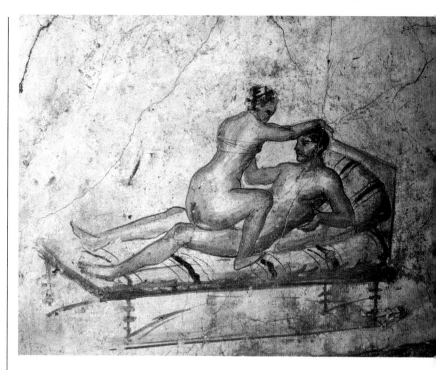

Amaseia, writing in the 5th century AD, commented on the Mysteries:

> *Is there not performed the descent*
> *into darkness, the venerated congress of*
> *the Hierophant with the priestess,*
> *of him alone with her alone?*
> *Are not the torches extinguished and*
> *does not the vast and*
> *countless assemblage believe that*
> *in what is done by the two in the*
> *darkness is their salvation?*

The power and resonance of these ceremonies and their attendant beliefs was considerable. Historians tell us that these rites were performed for nearly 2,000 years at Eleusis, and were only officially eradicated in the 4th century AD. However, there is some evidence that Greek peasants were still paying homage to the Great Mother goddess as late as the 19th century.

ABOVE *A Pompeian fresco of love-making reveals the uninhibited attitudes once prevalent in both Ancient Greek and Roman societies.*

BELOW *This Cretan bull's head represents male sexual energy and may be connected to the worship of Dionysus.*

RIGHT *Fresco showing a
procession at Knossos,
Crete. The young men
flank a joyful priestess.
Minoan culture remains
mysterious, but seems to
have focused on the goddess
as an elegant force
of nature.*

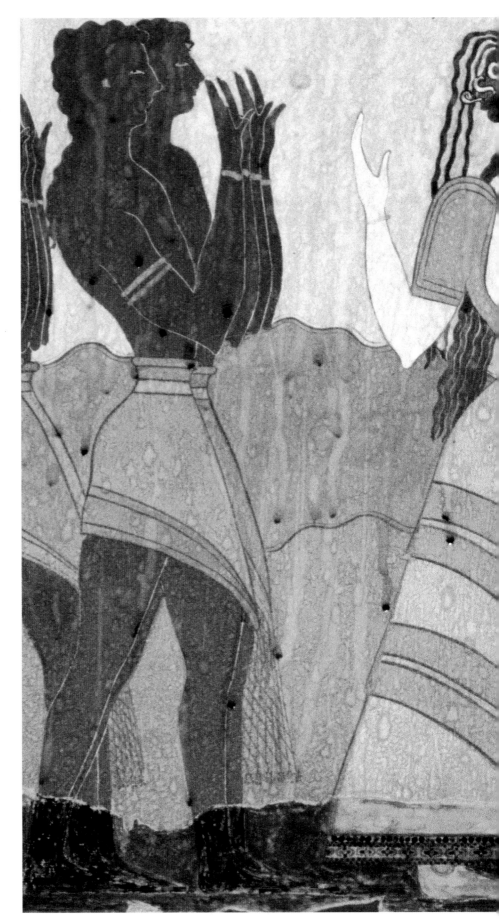

♦ ♦ ♦
DIONYSUS AND THE
MAENADS
♦ ♦ ♦

The multi-faceted figure of Dionysus, god of ecstasy, god of the vine and god of grain, is found in various forms all over the Middle East. As a baby at Eleusis he symbolized rebirth; as an adult god his cult was based on the theme of an endless cycle of death and regeneration, and his sacred rites were bloody, orgiastic and abandoned. His origins are possibly prehistoric, for he is a shamanic figure whose survival in Ancient Greece bears witness to his archetypal power.

Indra Sinha, an expert on classical and medieval Indian literature, writes, 'The connection between Indian Siva and Greek Dionysus, indeed their complete identification, was long ago acknowledged by Greek and Indian alike... in particular, they pointed to the similarity of the Bacchic processions with drums and cymbals to the dances of the Sydrakoi'[80] (an ancient tribe encountered by Alexander the Great in India).

Dionysus, carrying his phallic staff tipped with a pine cone *(thyrsus)*, and accompanied by a distinctly Eastern panther or tiger, roamed the forests and mountains. His priestesses, the Maenads or bacchantes, were wild women indeed – their divinely-inspired frenzies struck terror into the hearts of men for they were said to hunt and dismember animals, and sometimes human beings, with their bare hands. These rites celebrated the dismemberment of the god himself, and his inevitable regeneration.

In true tantric fashion, Dionysus intoxicated his followers. As Robert Calasso writes: 'This is Dionysus. He arrives, unexpected, and possesses.'[81] His

sexual nature was anarchic, and he was also known as the 'lord of the female sex'. The fact that Dionysus is always associated with women shows that he is also a son or lover of the earlier great goddess and requires her for his regeneration. Seated next to bright, logical Apollo on Mount Olympus, he symbolizes the vibrant and disturbing forces which oppose rational thought and behaviour: 'Dionysus' phallus... doesn't intoxicate to promote growth; yet, growth sustains intoxication, as the stem of a goblet holds up the wine.'[82] And just as Apollo is to the eternal sun, so the dying and rising Dionysus is to the waxing and waning moon.

EVA PRIMA PANDORA

Such forces not only possess arche-typal meaning, but are also capable of transformation into enlightening experi-ences as Professor E R Dodds' comments on Euripedes' *The Bacchae* reveal: '... we ignore at our peril the demand of the human spirit for Dionysiac experience. For those who do not close their minds against it, such experience can be a source of spiritual power and eudemonia. But those who repress the demand in themselves or refuse its satisfaction to others, transform it by their act into a power of disintegra-tion and destruction.'[83]

LEFT *Eva Prima Pandora by Jean Cousin the Elder (1490–1560). It is a medieval image inspired by the potency of the Greek myth.*

CHAPTER 9

The Goddess and the Roman Empire

FAR RIGHT *A naked bacchante, follower of Bacchus, dances with cymbals. Bacchus is the Roman personification of Dionysus.*

The 'glory that was Rome' endured for ten centuries, eventually encompassing a far-flung empire. In spiritual matters the Romans were both tolerant and pragmatic, adopting and adapting the gods and goddesses they found in other lands, finding sympathetic similarities between cross-cultural mythic figures, and rarely imposing their own forms of worship upon those they conquered. Consequently, myriad cults flourished under the Romans, including the widespread cult of Isis, the supreme Egyptian goddess, and Cybele, an Anatolian goddess of great antiquity. Both these cults spread to France, where Cybele became the ruling deity of the city of Lyons, while Isis was venerated in Paris for many centuries. Other deities were appropriated from the Greeks – Dionysus became Bacchus, Aphrodite became Venus, Demeter became Ceres, and so on.

Both Isis and Cybele were especially popular with female devotees. Both cults required periods of ritual celibacy, but also included distinctly erotic festivals and ceremonies. Many of the priestesses of Isis were totally celibate by choice, but the cult also contained erotic elements and more than a hint of sacred prostitution. Juvenal (a Roman satirist c 60–130 AD) commented that her priestesses were 'no better than bawds' and that Isis herself was one the Roman whores' favourite deities.

In sexual matters the Romans appear to have been equally broadminded, verging on the degenerate in the case of numerous emperors. The Victorian historian William Sanger wrote of them: 'It requires no small research to discover a single character in the long list... who was not stained by the grossest habits.'

Transvestism and the secular prostitution of both sexes were accepted as part of everyday life in the empire, with a number of emperors favouring women's dress, including the notorious Nero, Commodus, and Elagabalus who particularly enjoyed dressing up as the beautiful goddess Venus.

THE CHARMS OF VENUS

Venus, the Latin name for Aphrodite, comes from a noun meaning delight, charm, or attraction. In its most ancient derivation, it stems from the verb 'to venerate': 'primitively signified as the sacral act of alluring or enticing something from beyond mankind's power.'[84] Venus retained her association with Eros, although he lost much of his original power and came to be commonly depicted as a mischievous winged boy, Venus's son Cupid.

As a Roman goddess Venus was patroness of gardens, vineyards, love, nature and prostitutes. Venus Volgivava (Venus the Streetwalker) was one of her more colourful names. Her fading links with sacred sexual practices were honoured at the temple of Venus Erycina, just outside the city of Rome. Its design copied that of the original temple to Venus on Mt Eryx in Sicily, a shrine where sacred prostitution prospered for centuries.

On 23 and 25 April every year, prostitutes of both sexes, together with their children, and pimps, gathered at the temple to acknowledge Venus Erycina as their patroness, and venerate her. As profane prostitution flourished, the precincts of this temple became famous as a 'red light district'.

RIGHT *The Triumph of Venus by Francesco Podesti (19th century). Venus-Aphrodite represents an enduring female archetype.*

CYBELE – MAGNA MATER

Mother of all the gods
the mother of mortals
Sing of her
for me, Muse,
daughter of mighty Zeus,
a clear song

She loves the clatter of rattles
the din of kettle drums
and she loves the wailing of flutes

and also she loves the howling of wolves
and the growling of bright-eyed lions.[85]

Cybele, also named Magna Mater (Great Mother) by the Romans, was a fierce and terrible goddess. Her death-dealing aspect and love of noise and blood sacrifice are reminiscent of the Indian goddess Kali. As mother of the gods and all living things, worship of Cybele extended all over Asia Minor and into Western Europe. It was brought to Anatolia by the Phrygians in the 13th century BC, but seems to have been a widespread cult with links to Lydia (in southern Turkey) where she was also called Cybele, and to Mesopotamia where her name was Kubaba ('mistress of doves' – a bird sacred to Venus/Aphrodite because of its overtly affectionate mating behaviour).

Cybele's totemic creature was the lion or leopard, and she was accompanied by her son/lover the shepherd-boy Attis, who – like all ancient consorts – was sacrificed and regenerated annually. Cybele was brought to Rome on the advice of the Sibylline Books on 4 April 204 BC, at a time when Rome was

under severe threat of invasion from Hannibal's army. These books, records of prophecies spoken by the legendary female seers, were consulted by the Romans, just as the Greeks had consulted the Oracle at Delphi. Cybele became the mother goddess who must be brought to Rome if an invading army were to be defeated. Her image was duly carried with all pomp and ceremony to Rome. Some years later, Hannibal was defeated, and the goddess assured of an honoured place in the city.

Attis, as Cybele's consort, is one of the many vegetation gods who must die and be regenerated as a symbol of eternal life. The priests of Cybele castrated themselves with sickle-shaped knives or flints in honour of their fierce goddess

ABOVE *Anatolian Cybele, a fierce goddess*

FAR LEFT *Venus with Cupid the Honey Thief by Lucas Cranach*

BELOW *Attis and Cybele, who sits in a chariot drawn by lions*

ABOVE *The Discovery of the True Cross by Johann Georg Rudolphi. It relates the legend of former Roman prostitute St Helena.*

and the story of Attis's fall from grace. In the myth, Attis was loved by Cybele, who ordered him to remain faithful to her – or celibate in some versions. But he was tempted to betray her with a tree nymph. Once his lust was assuaged, he realized what he had done and was driven mad by remorse.

As he bled to death, violets sprang from his blood, and he was transformed into an evergreen tree, usually depicted as a pine tree. The tree, decorated with violets, was a central motif in the Mysteries of Cybele, while the phallic pine-cone became a symbol of Attis – echoing the pine-cone on the thyrsus of Dionysus. No Roman was allowed to become a priest of Cybele.

He mangled, too, his
body with a sharp stone, and trailed his
long hair in the filthy dust; and his cry
was 'I have deserved it! With my blood I
pay the penalty that is my due. Ah,
perish the parts that were my ruin!… He
retrenched the burden of his groin, and of
a sudden was bereft of every sign of
manhood.
His madness set an example, and still his
unmanly ministers cut their vile members
while they toss their hair.[86]

The principal rites of Cybele and Attis were as bloody and ecstatic as those of Dionysus. Her festival was called the Megalensia, or Great Mother's Games. One of its central features, the Taurobolium, was the sacrifice and ritual castration of a bull, who symbolized Attis. Initiates were drenched in its blood, which was believed to redeem them for after this ritual they were said to have been reborn. In Rome, Attis 'died' on 24 March, the Day of Blood, when frenzied male devotees castrated themselves. His regeneration the following day was celebrated by the Hilaria, a great carnival attended by loud music, feasting, general revelry and abandoned sexual licence.

♦ ♦ ♦

FLORA AND THE FEVERS OF LOVE

♦ ♦ ♦

In 46 BC the date of the Hilaria was moved to 1 May in line with the Julian calendar. This date still remains significant all over Europe as the date of the great spring festivals, and in Rome it became known as the festival of the Roman goddess Flora, the Floralia. Her festival was, like the Hilaria which predated it, a riotous celebration of sexuality, life, dancing and music.

But this was by no means the highlight of the Roman year. Another erotic spring festival celebrated by the Romans was the Lupercalia, a celebration sacred to Juno Februata, goddess of the fevers of love. On this day young men sent love notes to women, the origin of Valentine's Day cards centuries later. Many men also paraded in the streets wearing women's clothing, probably in honour of the feminine principle behind the festivities. These customs continued into Christian times, when St Valentine was invented by the Church in an attempt to appropriate and sanctify proceedings.

The aid of Juno (the Greek Hera) was also sought in matters of love. Catullus (87–47 BC) describes a young woman praying to 'Juno of the birthday', asking the goddess to grant her the love of a particular man.

BELOW *Juno, known in Greece as Hera, was goddess of marriage and, as Juno Februata, goddess of the fevers of love.*

To-day she is thine wholly;
most joyfully she has decked
herself for thee, to stand before
thy altar a sight for all to see…
They are making offering to thee,
holy goddess, thrice with cake
and thrice with wine…
She burns as the altar burns
with the darting flames,
nor, even though she might,
would she be whole. Be grateful,
Juno, so that, when the next
year comes, this love,
now of long standing, may be
there unchanged to meet
their prayers.[87]

The Bacchantes, too, represent one of the many links between Rome and Ancient Greece. They were votaries of the god Bacchus, the Latin name for Dionysus. Bacchus, a god of wine and ecstasy, was also originally a god of women, although his mythic followers later included goat-footed satyrs – symbols of virile masculine libido. His wild rumbustious revels, the Bacchanalia, were banned in Rome in 186 BC, only to be reintroduced in the 1st century AD.

♦♦♦

SIBYLS AND VIRGINS

♦♦♦

Two of the most important Roman spiritual/sexual connections with the archaic past are embodied in the long-standing traditions of the Vestal Virgins, and the legendary sibyls, or prophetesses. The Romans had consulted the sibyls and their writings for centuries, and in this respect there is a link with Greece and the Delphic Oracle. The first sibyl was said to have been the daughter of a snake woman (the Lamia) and Zeus. One legend says that the Lamia had a

luxurious palace at Corinth, which perhaps connects her sensuous and seductive persona to the temple of Aphrodite in the very same city.

Certainly, the sibyls were often young, and as a prelude to prophecy would enact a passionate ecstatic trance during which they communed with the god Apollo. Virgil (70–19 BC) offers this description in his *Aeneid*:

'Now is the time to consult
the oracle. Lo, the god,
the god!' and as she spoke her
face and colour changed,
her hair fell in disorder,
her bosom heaved and panted,
her heart swelled with wild
frenzy; she seemed to become
taller, her voice no longer
sounded human; the god was
near her, touching her with
his breath.

FAR LEFT *The goddess Flora was honoured with riotous springtime festivities, dating back to the earliest sacred sexual rites known.*

LEFT *The goddess Hera, wife of Zeus, was transmuted into Juno by the Romans.*

ABOVE *This Roman mosaic shows Dionysus, one of the many Greek deities adopted by the Romans.*

The sibyls favoured caves as their dwelling places, linking them and their primal serpentine origins to the ancient and sacred uterine homes of the archaic goddesses. The Vestal Virgins' temple also symbolized the womb of the goddess, for it was round, signifying earth and the feminine principle. The temple was roofed in bronze, and contained no image of the goddess because, 'Vesta is the same as the Earth; under both of them is a perpetual fire; the earth and the hearth are symbols of the home.'[88]

The six Vestal Virgins were the specially-chosen priestesses of the hearth goddess, Vesta (in Greek Hestia). Their sacred duty was to keep alight the flames which burned on her hearth, and which symbolized the living heart of the city of Rome. Their legal powers were reminiscent of those enjoyed by the prostitute-priestesses of Sumeria, Babylon and Greece, but they were supposed to be celibate during their traditional 30 years of service. According to Ovid, this was because of Vesta's own virgin nature: 'Conceive of Vesta as naught but the living flame, and you see that no bodies are born of flame. Rightly, therefore, is she a virgin who neither gives nor takes seeds, and she loves companions in her virginity.'[89]

The Vestal Virgins were selected from the most influential families by the resident high priest, the Pontifex Maximus, when they were children between the ages of six and ten. Plutarch wrote that, 'during the first decade they are to learn their duties, during the second to perform the duties they have learned, and during the third to teach others these duties. Then, the thirty years being now passed, any one who wishes has liberty to marry and adopt a different mode of life.' Retaining their virginity sometimes proved difficult, and led to numerous scandals. In 114 BC a temple was dedicated to Venus Verticordia (Venus, Turner of Hearts) to celebrate the acquittal of two of the Vestal Virgins who had been accused of breaking their vows of celibacy. But any priestess found guilty suffered a horrible fate – she was ceremonially walled up alive in a small chamber beneath the city walls.

BELOW *A 19th-century rendition of a voluptuous sybil in pensive mood.*

ABOVE *Emperor Constantine I and his mother, St Helena (Yilani Church, Cappadocia)*

FAR RIGHT *A Vestal Virgin bearing the eternal flame*

Sacred and profane sexuality co-existed in Roman culture. Prostitution bore little stigma, although whores were supposed to be registered with an official, the *aedile*. Amongst the numerous categories of trade on offer, remnants of sacred sexual rituals could still be discerned. The frenzies of the Maenads were echoed by the wailing cries of the *lupae*, or she-wolves, who howled like wolves to attract prospective clients.

Timeless links between sexual ecstasy and death were embodied by the *busturariae*, women who worked in Rome's graveyards and had intercourse on the tombstones, but also offered their services as funeral mourners. The clearest connection between sacred and profane must be the *aelicariae*, girls who sold little cakes baked in the shape of male and female genitals which were intended as sacrificial offerings to Venus.

Two former Roman courtesans found their previous career no hindrance to power and glory. Theodora, actress, comedienne, dancer and prostitute rose from utter obscurity to become Empress of the Eastern Roman Empire. She was the daughter of a dancer and a bear keeper at the Hippodrome in Constantinople. A Roman senator, Justinian, became infatuated with her to the extent that he begged his uncle, the Emperor Justinian, to revoke the law which forbade senators to marry prostitutes. Theodora duly became Empress in the 6th century AD, whereupon she influenced her husband to amend the laws governing prostitution, and established a convent for penitent whores. Her mosaic portrait at the church of San

Some historians, including Barbara Walker,[90] assert that the Vestal Virgins underwent a form of secret marriage ceremony with the Pontifex Maximus, who initiated them into their role as 'brides' of the city, and the phallic deity of the Palladium. Another hint of sacred sexual rituals comes from the Vestals' springtime custom of casting little dolls into the River Tiber, just as the body of Aphrodite's lover, Adonis, was cast into rivers or the sea as part of his death and regeneration.

ABOVE *Mosaic portrait (Church of S. Vitale, Ravenna, Italy). The Empress Theodora began as a prostitute and became a devout Christian.*

FAR RIGHT *The virginal hearth goddess Vesta, with an offering of food*

Vitale, in Ravenna, Italy, shows her resplendent with jewels – as befitted her station in life. Its presence there tacitly acknowledges a power that transcends her origins and former profession, and once again presents the image of a prostitute inside a temple.

♦♦♦
ST HELENA
♦♦♦

The formidable mother of the Emperor Constantine, St Helena may have used her considerable influence on her son, urging him to accept and condone Christianity. The 12th-century historian, Geoffrey of Monmouth, put forward the claim that she was a British woman,

daugher of King Ceol of Colchester, and the Welsh *Mabinogion* describes her as a princess, bride of the self-appointed Roman emperor, Magnus Maximus, who was led to her by a dream. She was certainly a former courtesan and became a zealous and devout woman who, aged 70, made the pilgrimage to Jerusalem in search of the true cross. Legend says that she found three crosses – one for Christ, and one for each of the thieves crucified with him – in a crypt beneath the ancient temple of Aphrodite. To divine which of the crosses was the holy relic she ordered a corpse to be laid on each one. The true cross restored the corpse to life.

This fable contains so many interlocking strands of pagan goddess worship – the holy prostitute, the phallic regenerative cross, the presence of Aphrodite – that it is hardly surprising to learn that it was never reported as an actual event at the time (328 AD). Indeed, throughout the complex labyrinth of myth, fable, fairy tale and legend – which grows ever more dense as the centuries proceed – the same motifs continue to prevail.

ABOVE *Pompeian fresco showing a figure*
thought to be the god Mercury in aerial embrace
with a woman

The Virgin, the Whore and the Demon Queen

For I am the first and the last.
I am the honoured one
  and the scorned one.
I am the whore and the holy one.
I am the wife and the virgin.
I am (the mother) and the daughter.
I am the members of my mother…
I am the silence that is incomprehensible
  and the idea whose remembrance
  is frequent.
I am the voice whose sound is manifold
  and the word whose appearance
  is multiple.
I am the utterance of my name.

'THE THUNDER, PERFECT MIND'[91]

Images of the divine feminine, and the sexual secrets which accompanied them, had existed for thousands of years. And while centuries of patriarchal morals and mores have eroded the status of living women quite efficiently, they could not so easily eradicate the presence of the goddess and her mysteries.

The strength and potential numinosity of sexuality had been acknowledged and celebrated for millennia. And the figure of the goddess of a thousand names and her lover was rooted in the hearts and minds of their worshippers. These resonant images reflected an idealization of human sexual love, the mysteries of procreation, and the transforming qualities of pleasure. Yet Judeo-Christian dogma sought to change these beliefs – literally and symbolically 'flying in the face of Nature'.

So what happened to this vast body of belief and spiritual practice? It transformed itself in numerous subtle ways. It appeared in ecclesiastical carvings; in symbolic paintings; in legends, stories and fairy tales; and lived on in esoteric lore and sanitized pagan ceremonies.

The image of the divine feminine endured (in part) in the Virgin Mary – purity incarnate. But what about the Black Madonnas? What do they signify? The tangle of superstitions and fables surrounding such figures as Mary Magdalene, the Queen of Sheba, Eve and Lilith, suggests a profound dissatisfaction with the Virgin alone. Similarly, the new monotheisms sought to control male sexuality. Again, the old fertility gods – vegetation deities to a man – found a way in. Like smoke beneath a door, their images could not, would not, be banished. And so the Green Man, a resoundingly pagan figure, began to be depicted in churches all over Europe. Overall, despite the moral censure of the established Church, ordinary people did not relinquish their beliefs easily. The erosion of paganism, and its celebration of fertility and sexual pleasure, took place over many centuries. Apparent success was achieved by the 19th century in Europe, the Near and Middle East, and the United States. However, even the most cursory probing beneath the veneer of respectability will reveal a flourishing sexual sub-culture – albeit debased and hypocritical. The Church of England accorded the Virgin Mary far less prominence than the Roman Catholics, and by the 19th century the concept of the divine feminine had reached an all-time low in Protestant circles. This whole period is marked in Europe by the effects of the Industrial Revolution. As people flocked to the cities to earn their living, rural communities began to decline and this collective separation from Nature can only have exacerbated the undermining of the divine feminine image, rooted as it is in the cycles of the seasons and the

ABOVE *The Black Madonna of Czestochowa, one of the mysterious black Madonnas found in European Churches, with links to much older goddess figures*

FAR RIGHT *A symbolic rendition of Madonna and child (Scenes of The Life of Jesus by Beato Angelico)*

'animal' instincts. It is interesting that this period culminated with a time when women began to assert themselves, demanding the right to vote, and to be recognized as equals.

The history of the Virgin Mary as icon can be linked with women's struggle to be recognized and accepted. It was at Ephesus, where the awesome figure of many-breasted Artemis had reigned supreme for so long, that the Virgin Mary was finally accorded her title, *Theotokos* (Mother of God) in 431 AD. The cult of the Virgin Mary flourished throughout the Middle Ages and beyond. She assimilated the qualities and titles of the goddesses before her: for example, Queen of Heaven (Ishtar and Isis, among the many), the Blessed Virgin (Juno), Stella Maris (Isis), and Queen of Hell (Persephone, Erishkigal). She was, and still is, seen as all-merciful, as the beneficent mediatrix between human beings and their god.

The one crucial aspect of the goddesses that she did not assimilate or embody was their sensuality, their uninhibited sexuality. Even her motherhood was played down, or doubted, by the early Church fathers. Epiphanius said '... let no one worship Mary'. The sexual feminine, by now seen as 'sinful' and accursed, was carried by a curious mixture of figures: Eve, the first woman; the exotic Queen of Sheba; the demonic Lilith; and above all, the archetypal repentant whore and tart with a heart of gold, Mary Magdalene. The sexuality of male divinity was also under attack as a manifestation of the devil, but masculine potency and phallic fertility were not to be entirely denied, as the myriad images of the mysterious Green Man in European churches bear witness.

♦ ♦ ♦
EVE AND LILITH,
OUTRAGED OUTCASTS
♦ ♦ ♦

As we have seen, the authorized Bible story names Eve as Adam's wife in the Garden of Eden. But according to earlier Hebrew tradition, Adam's first wife was called Lilith and she was created at the same time – suggesting equality of the sexes.

When Lilith left the Garden (see page 136) she became a dangerous and demonic outcast, a screech owl or night monster – symbolic of repressed feminine instinct and sexuality. Eve, created to be less troublesome than Lilith, was deceived and lured into temptation by the serpent. Ironically, this creature is an ancient and universal goddess symbol; its presence represents the demonization of the old order.

The serpent persuaded Eve to eat the fruit of the Tree of Knowledge of Good and Evil, and to share this with her husband. This so enraged God that not only did he cast the hapless pair out of the Garden, but for good measure cursed them for all eternity.

Gnostic texts, however, tell a different tale. They refer to Eve as the 'Mother of all Living' who created Adam to be her consort, while early Jewish traditions support the suggestion that the serpent *was* Eve, and the mother of both Adam and Eve. Similarly, the prophetic Greek and Roman sibyls were said to be descended from the primal snake-woman, or Lamia, of Greek myth.

ABOVE *Eve by Lucas Cranach (1472–1553). Eve, the fruit of knowledge and the wise serpent symbolize the presence of the ancient past within a new religion.*

FAR LEFT *Mary Magdalene, by Antonio Zanchi. A powerful Gnostic embodiment of feminine sexuality, she is conventionally shown as a penitent figure.*

RIGHT *A Green Man,
(Norwich Cathedral,
England) 12th century*

BELOW *A Green Man
roof boss looks down on the
congregation (Canterbury
Cathedral, England).*

While Eve commonly represents the subjugation of the feminine, Lilith symbolizes rebellion, rage and an untamed sexual nature. Her origins are very ancient; she is sometimes known as the 'hand of Inanna', who encouraged men to come and worship at the goddess's temple. She is also, variously, a Sumerian demon of the storm, a seductive succuba, the daughter or bride of Satan, and Adam's clandestine lover or first wife.

Lilith is always, significantly, homeless, and wanders about between the domains of Heaven and Earth. *The Alphabet of Ben Sira,* an 11th-century kabbalistic work, says that Adam and Lilith were once an androgynous being with equal rights and substance. But this ideal state could not last: 'Adam and Lilith never found peace together. She… refused to lie beneath him in sexual intercourse, basing her claim for equality on the fact that each had been created

from earth. When Lilith saw that Adam would overpower her, she uttered the ineffable name of God and flew up into the air of the world. Eventually, she dwelt in a cave in the desert on the shores of the Red Sea. There she engaged in unbridled promiscuity, consorted with lascivious demons, and gave birth to hundreds of Lilim, or demonic babies, daily.'

In the oldest known image of Lilith, a Sumerian bas-relief, she is shown with wings and bird's feet, flanked by owls and standing on a pair of lions – creatures sacred to Ishtar and Cybele. Her powers are in the ascendant during the night, at the time of the new moon, and during the dark of the moon. The Kabbalists were afraid of her power and said she adorned herself 'like a harlot' in a scarlet dress, glittering with jewellery and armed with a cup of poisonous wine with which to entice and seduce her innocent male victims. However, they also pictured her as a stage of initiation on the Tree of Life, and in the 13th

century described her as 'a ladder on which one can ascend to the rungs of prophecy'.

The Gnostic Mandaeans, followers of John the Baptist, say that Lilith is the daughter of the King and Queen of the Underworld, who marries the King of Light or Knowledge and bears him a son who has knowledge of both worlds. In the Pyrenees she is associated with the legend of Noctiluca, queen of the night-hags, and the Black Fairies of the Pyrenees who, Lilith-like, would seize and ravish any young men foolish enough to travel alone in the mountains by night. In the Pyrenean cathedral of St Bertrand de Comminges, Lilith has found her way into church: a carving there depicts a winged, bird-footed woman giving birth to a Dionysian figure, a Green Man.

♦ ♦ ♦

THE GREEN MAN

♦ ♦ ♦

The Green Man, disgorger of vegetation, aspect of the horned god of the Celts, and direct descendant of Dionysus, appears in numerous Christian churches all over Europe. However he is shown — sometimes alone, sometimes beneath an image of the Virgin and Child, sometimes young and robust, sometimes old and forbidding — his image is one of death and rebirth and he is linked to the mystery religions of the ancient world.

The curious story of Bishop Nicetus (526–566 AD) may mark the dawn of the Green Man's tacit acceptance into the Christian Church. When Bishop Nicetus was rebuilding the great cathedral at Trier, in what is now Germany, he, like many other early builders, used the stones which were already to hand on the sites of pagan temples, in this case a Roman temple at Am Herrenbrunnchen. Amongst these were some vast composite capitals, each displaying red and yellow leaf masks, the foliate heads of the Green Man. These columns were prominently placed in the reconstructed cathedral for all to see (they were walled up during the Middle Ages, but rediscovered in the 19th century).

BELOW *Lilith, Adam's first wife, shown as a winged goddess with bird's feet (2000–1800 BC)*

This vegetation deity has a lengthy and complex history in ecclesiastical art and iconography. In his book *The Green Man*, William Anderson points out that there is a '...close analogy between man's sexual nature and the writhing vegetation', citing various examples of frankly sexual imagery at Chartres Cathedral in France, at Lincoln Cathedral, and in Romanesque churches in France, Spain and Britain. 'Male and female figures display their genitalia often grossly exaggerated, couples copulate or indulge in homosexual practices. In numbers of these examples these figures are associated with vegetation and are interspersed with heads or ... figures of Green Men.'

♦ ♦ ♦

THE QUEEN OF SHEBA AND THE SONG OF SOLOMON

♦ ♦ ♦

I am black, but comely,
O ye daughters of Jerusalem

SONG OF SOLOMON 1:5

The Queen of Sheba, like the Green Man, is also associated with Lilith and the goddess of love. The Old Testament of the Bible tells the story of the visit of the Queen of Sheba to wise King Solomon 'with a very great train, with camels that bare spices, and very much gold, and precious stones' (I Kings 10:2). This tale clearly refers to a time when the worship of a male father god, Yahweh, had not yet totally superseded the older practice of venerating the goddess. Solomon's senile indulgence towards his 700 wives and 300 concubines is blamed for his weakness in abandoning Yahweh and turning back to Ashtoreth, another name for Ishtar, the

Whore of Babylon. The Queen of Sheba herself represents both the goddess and the culture which venerated her. As Barbara Walker writes, 'Solomon's reign and deeds must be interpreted as a collection of legends from Egypt, Phoenicia, and especially from southern Arabia, the land of Sheba, where a true Golden Age was flourishing under a succession of matriarchal queens.'[92]

The seductive Queen of Sheba, or 'Queen of the South', proved to be a compelling figure in medieval legends and allegories. She was said to be one of the sibyls, foretelling Christ's crucifixion, and, like Lilith, she had a webbed foot, or the hairy legs of an ass or a goat which Solomon was able to make human through his magical powers. As Marina Warner comments, '... in the Judeo-Christian tradition, sexuality offered the principal site of danger'. The Queen's deformity and its subsequent healing therefore 'not only signifies her recognition of the true god, but announces the possible miraculous redemption of her femaleness.'[93]

Other fables say that this exotic couple became lovers or were married and produced a son, an heir to all their wealth and wisdom. Certainly, a record of a sacred marriage remains in the Bible, a fragment of tender love poetry which later authorities claimed was an allegory of Christ's marriage to the body of the Church. The so-called 'Song of Solomon', or 'Song of Songs', celebrates the distinctly erotic love between 'the rose of Sharon, and the lily of the valleys' and her beloved, named as Solomon, who was crowned by his mother (the priestess) 'in the day of the gladness of his heart', the day of his sacred wedding to the black queen.

FAR LEFT *A modern painting by the painter Robert Burns illustrating a verse from the Song of Solomon*

ABOVE *Solomon and the Queen of Sheba from the Winchester Bible*

This beautiful and sensual poem opens with the bride's command: 'Let him kiss me with the kisses of his mouth: for thy love is better than wine' (Song of Solomon 1:2). The 'Shulamite', the bride of this poem, praises her lover in the most unequivocal terms: 'A bundle of myrrh is my well-beloved unto me; he shall lie all night betwixt my breasts.' Her consort then invites her to come to him in the spring, the traditional season for honouring the goddess's most abundant and beautiful fecundity:

Rise up, my love, my fair one, and come away. For, lo, the winter is past, the rain is over and gone; the flowers appear on the earth; the time of the singing of birds is come, and the voice of the turtle is heard in our land.
The fig tree putteth forth her green figs, and the vines with the tender grape give a good smell. Arise, my love, my fair one, and come away.

SONG OF SOLOMON 2: 10–12

It is this poetic combination of burgeoning nature and erotic invitation which embodies the essence of sacred sexuality. It is an approach which has much to offer us today in a world which is becoming increasingly sterile.

RIGHT *The Great Harlot seated on a seven-headed monster represents a biblical interpretation of earlier myths of Ishtar, the Mesopotamian goddess.*

♦ ♦ ♦
THE BLACK MADONNA AND THE MAGDALENE
♦ ♦ ♦

*The companion of the Saviour is
Mary Magdalene.
But Christ loved her more
than all the disciples and used
to kiss her often on her mouth.
The rest of the disciples were
offended by it… They said to him
'Why do you love her more
than all of us?' The Saviour
answered and said to them,
'Why do I not love you
as I love her?'*

GNOSTIC GOSPEL OF PHILIP [94]

The Black Madonna may represent the ultimate chthonic goddess image, the Shulamite bride of the Song of Solomon. Indeed, there is a statue of the Black Madonna at Tindari in Sicily bearing the inscription 'nigra sum sed formosa' (I am black, but comely). Like the Green Man, she is also found also in Chartres Cathedral, where she is called Our Lady Under the Earth. Places where the Black Madonna is venerated, often as a miracle worker, are frequently linked to the cult of Mary Magdalene – repentant harlot of biblical myth, and Christ's beloved companion according to Gnostic scriptures. The Gnostics say that Jesus and Mary Magdalene were lovers

ABOVE *The Whore of Babylon, from the Luther Bible, c 1530*

ABOVE *The Black Virgin (18th century), a figure*
who suggests secret knowledge within the heart of the Church

who withdrew to a mountain where their sexual raptures revealed to the disciples what must be done so that 'we might have life'.

Legend tells us that Mary Magdalene sailed to France, alighting at Les Saintes-Maries-de-la-Mer. She was accompanied by various other biblical figures, including Mary Salome, Mary the mother of the apostle James, and Sara, her black Egyptian maid – now the special saint of the Romany people and widely believed to be an aspect of Isis. Mary Magdalene herself is said to have been a high priestess of Ishtar or Isis, and to have been the mother of Jesus's son. The stories and fables surrounding her contain many intricate layers and many esoteric hints as to her true origins. Whoever she was, whether living woman and/or composite goddess figure,

her image, like that of the Black Virgin, has been venerated throughout the orthodox Christian and less orthodox Gnostic religions.

The Magdalene, The Green Man, Lilith and the Black Virgin are gloriously subversive figures, with strong links to Gnostic heresies, Eastern heterodox groups, and Jewish and Arabic mystical traditions. The learned and educated followers of these various teachings not only kept the old traditions alive, but also developed complex philosophies of their own within the context of these traditions. Meanwhile, the vivid visual and written imagery inspired by these symbolic figures – present within the heart of the Christian Church – continued to ensure that the essence of the great goddess and her consort was not lost and gone forever.

CHAPTER 11

The Cauldron of Celtic Regeneration

The Celts remain an elusive people, for they left no written record. Celtic legends, rituals and myths were sung and spoken, preserved only by a resonant oral tradition unimaginable to us today. Centuries later, monks laboured to record these tales; other information comes from Roman observers, who noted that the Celts were polygamous. Striking stone carvings, and objects ritually buried or cast into bogs also offer images of the Celts' sacred world. Their beliefs, intertwined with Anglo-Saxon and classical influences, form the basis of the pagan calendar, with its celebrations and robust attitudes towards sexual pleasure and freedom.

Classical commentators refer to a variety of tribes as *keltoi*; however, within this group, linked more by language than racial origins, are the Welsh, Irish, Scots-Gaelic, Manx, Cornish and Breton peoples. These communities 'did not derive from a single community of continental Celts...'[95] Moreover, the Celtic languages divide into two branches – Irish, Scottish and Manx (categorized as Goidelic); and Welsh, Cornish, and Breton (categorized as Brittonic).

Certain themes, such as magical regenerative cauldrons, female priestesses, magical queens and supernatural islands, are found in numerous narratives, but Celtic gods and goddesses are, above all, spirits of nature, many of them local deities inhabiting a lake, a tree or a special cave.

◆ ◆ ◆

THE ENCHANTED REALMS

◆ ◆ ◆

Caesar named only one goddess of the Celts. He called her Minerva, and identified her domain as arts and crafts. He obviously associated her with a goddess from his own pantheon, although Celtic goddess figures were connected with the whole of life in a way that Roman ones were not.

Fairy lore, although written down centuries later, offers some glimpses of Celtic beliefs and customs – a goddess and her consort, the horned hunter god, appear to have been familiar figures in this misty landscape. Fairy lore was originally part of the great, vibrant oral tradition, the threads of which are impossible to unravel. In Ireland, for example, fairies are said to this day to live inside the ancient barrows and burial mounds which were the holy places of the megalithic peoples.

The king o' fairy with his rout
Come to hunt him all about
With dim cry and blowing
And hounds also with him barking...
SIR ORFEO, C 1300 [96]

Fairies, and other beings of the enchanted realms, inhabited hills, forests and sacred springs all over Europe, places once sacred to the old goddess-centred earth religions. In Brittany, a poem told of the nine Korrigen, beautiful women robed in white, who danced around a fountain by the light of the full moon. By day, however, they were revealed as white-haired, red-eyed crones. Wise old women, like the priestesses of old, were also reputed to have secret shrines where they imparted magical knowledge to younger women. These skills included changing shapes, raising storms, and the 'rites of Venus' – or the arts of love, invariably sacred to the goddess of a thousand names.

Celtic goddesses seem to have commonly had three aspects – the moon's phases personified as the maiden, mother and crone. The number three, and multiplications of three, were considered magical, and many later stories contained beasts with three heads, three wishes, nine maidens, and so on. The Celtic goddesses also exhibited two contrasting aspects – beautiful and repulsive – which they could assume at will. This duality seems to symbolize the changeable forces of nature, so crucial to the well-being of early peoples, and perhaps the unpredictable nature of woman.

ABOVE *A 19th-century vision of a religious festival. The mysterious Celts inspired many later artists.*

Many fairy tales of Celtic origin tell how, under the correct magical circumstances, an ugly or deformed old crone is transformed into a beautiful maiden. There is something inescapably alchemical about this motif which hints at sacred sexual knowledge, while not presenting it directly. Indeed, while there is no evidence for a goddess of love in the sense of an Aphrodite figure, divine sexuality and fertility are undoubtedly celebrated in pagan Celtic festivals, folklore and legend. The creative forces of the earth itself, once venerated by the architects of the great stone circles and other

ABOVE *Minerva, the Roman goddess mistakenly named by Caesar as the goddess of the Celts*

megalithic monuments, can clearly be seen in the multiple fragments of Celtic culture that remain. These people lived their lives in a landscape which already contained awe-inspiring relics of former traditions, and it is hard to believe they were not influenced by them to some extent. Certainly, the Celtic gods and goddesses, like the ghosts and supernatural beings which superseded them, are frequently associated with water, sacred groves, and totemic creatures – notably the boar, deer, hare, horse and raven.

♦ ♦ ♦

THE HORNED GOD

♦ ♦ ♦

*The Goddess: Black the town yonder,
Black those that are in it,
I am the White Swan,
Queen of all living.*

*The God: I will voyage as God,
Like a stag, like a stallion,
Like a snake, like a King,
Stronger than any.*

ANONYMOUS GAELIC POEM [97]

ABOVE *Men-an-Tol (Cornwall, England). These sacred ancient stones symbolize male and female genitals.*

The most striking Celtic personification of masculine potency is Cernunnos, a shamanic figure whose origins are shrouded in antiquity. In her book *Shaman, The Wounded Healer*, Joan Halifax writes: 'The stag, reindeer, and

deer, the medium of magical transport for the shaman, is believed to be a mediator between heaven and earth. The antlers, symbolic of regeneration and growth because of the way they are renewed, are often associated with the Sacred Tree and the mysteries of death and rebirth.'[98] Images of shamans wearing antlers can be found all over the world, while the deer itself is associated in shamanic lore with healing, visionary trances, grace, and abundant fertility.

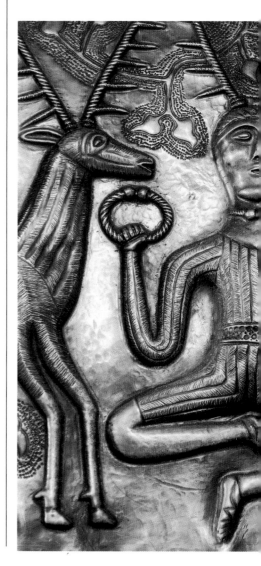

On the side of the Gundestrup Cauldron, Cernunnos, the great horned god, is depicted in a yogic cross-legged pose, grasping a ram-headed serpent which he is about to thrust into a ring. 'This beast is "more subject to magic spells than are other animals" as the *Malleus Maleficarum* puts it, linking it with the penis'.[99] The fertility-magic of the horned god was still being invoked in 19th-century England, as the following eye-witness account reveals:

The annual wakes at Abbot Bromley, a village on the borders of Needwood Forest, near Stafford, is celebrated by a curious survival from medieval times called the Horn-dance. Six deer-skulls with antlers, mounted on short poles, are carried about by men grotesquely attired, who caper to a lively tune, and make 'the deer', as the antlers are called, dance about. Another quaintly-dressed individual, mounted on a hobby-horse, is at hand with a whip, with which he lashes the deer every now and again in order to keep them moving. Meanwhile a sportsman with a bow and arrow makes believe to shoot the deer. The horn-dance used to take place on certain Sunday mornings at the main entrance to the parish church, when a collection was made for the poor. At the present day the horns are the property of the vicar for the time being, and are kept, with a bow and arrow and the frame of the hobby-horse, in the church's tower, together with a curious old pot for collecting money at the dance. It takes place now on the Monday after Wakes Sunday, which is the Sunday next to September 4th. The money is collected by a woman, probably Maid Marion; the archer is doubtless a representation of Robin Hood; and besides these characters there is a jester. Dr Cox has examined the horns, and pronounced them to be reindeer horns.'[100]

LEFT *The Celtic god Cernunnos with cult beasts, depicted on the Gundestrup Cauldron. This was found in Denmark and believed to be a rare example of Celtic art.*

Some 300 years before this account was written another antiquarian, one Dr Plot, had also examined these horns and come to the same conclusion. Although reindeer have been extinct in the British Isles since the 12th century, the Horned God continued to be commemorated – although the original reasons for the ritual dance had been forgotten. Ceremonies like the one above were often performed at Yuletide, during the twelve days of Christmas, formerly an important festival of death and rebirth. In 7 AD, Theodore, Archbishop of Canterbury, issued an edict against such pagan practices:

If anyone at the Kalends of January goes about as a stag or a bull; that is, making himself into a wild animal and dressing in the skin of a herd animal, and putting on the heads of beasts; those who in such wise transform themselves into the appearance of a wild animal, penance for three years because this is devilish.

LIBER POENITENTIALIS

◆ ◆ ◆

CELTIC PRIESTS AND PRIESTESSES

◆ ◆ ◆

The Druids, or Celtic priesthood, passed their esoteric traditions on by word of mouth and sharpness of memory. Knowledge passed down a long chain, originally thought to be female. Later, Druids included male and female initiates, and for this they were attacked by the Church authorities. Their ceremonies centred upon sacred groves, where they especially revered the mighty oak tree. Strabo,[101] one of the few early sources of information about Celtic customs, claims that orgiastic rites involving blood sacrifice took place in these groves, similar to those held in Greece.

An ancient fertility ritual described by Doreen Valiente perhaps offers a clue to the actual nature of these rites. A naked man and woman dance seven times around a large tree, 'preferably an oak', acting out a symbolic chase. On the seventh round the woman allows herself to be caught, and the couple make love beneath the tree. 'At the end of the rite, a leaf is plucked from the tree and moistened with the sexual fluids that have been mingled in the woman's vagina. This leaf is considered to be a powerful talisman…' [102]

Celtic tradition also included a number of exclusive sisterhoods, priestesses who were reminiscent of the Vestal Virgins in Rome. We can only guess at their activities, but one of their duties was to keep a sacred fire alight at their shrines. These shrines, such as one at Kildare in Ireland, were strictly forbidden to men. The name Kildare is identified with the goddess Kilda-Kele, later known as Brigit. Kelle was also a word meaning harlot, and is linked by scholars with the Indo-European goddess Kali. As Kelle, the goddess had an adoring consort, represented by three sacred colours – red for life and creative powers, white for preservation, and black for her rulership of death and destruction. Kelle was a druidic priest-name, now rendered Kelly – a common Irish surname.

♦ ♦ ♦
THE SPIRIT OF WATER
♦ ♦ ♦

Where fresh water runs
there runs spirit… for it comes from
the realm of the earth goddess and
bears her gifts. [103]

Wells, springs, rivers and lakes were sacred places to both Celts and the pagan people who came after them. Coventina (Mother of Covens) was one special goddess associated with them, as was Brigit or Bride in Ireland. For centuries many ancient wells were cared for by a female custodian who helped pilgrims enact the correct rituals. Many of these custodians seem to have been hereditary guardians, their links with the well quite possibly stretching back to pre-Christian times. Other sacred waters are traditionally haunted by a host of female spirits, white ladies, mermaids or fairies, strongly suggesting the submerged memory of a goddess.

The Irish story of Niall and his four brothers suggests that some kind of sacred sexual ritual was once associated with wells. These five men encountered

LEFT *Coventina, goddess of the sacred waters from which all life comes*

a hideous hag who was guarding a well. 'Her hair was like a wild horse's tail. Her foul teeth were visible from ear to ear and were such as would sever a branch of green oak. Her eyes were black, her nose crooked and spread. Her body was scrawny, spotted and diseased. Her shins were bent. Her knees and ankles were thick, her shoulders broad, her nails were green.' She demanded a kiss from each of the brothers in payment for the water from her well. But only Niall was bold enough. He embraced her, and became her lover – whereupon she was transformed. 'She was as white as the last snow in a hollow. Her arms were full and queenly, her fingers long and slender, her legs straight and gleaming… '[104]

The potent powers attributed to water evince the typical lack of division between all manifestations of magical energy found throughout the old religions. Healing, prophecy, cursing, fertility and sexuality were all associated with these places, as they were with the sacred groves and other wild places. Over the centuries ancient rituals invoking divine aid became folk customs, but traces of the old cults may still be discerned in these ceremonies. Many, for example, took place on the dates of Celtic festivals, especially on 1 or 12 May to celebrate the fertility feast of Beltane, or on Midsummer's Day, the time of the summer solstice celebrations. The holy wells, in particular, were places of pilgrimage on such days. They were decorated with fresh flowers and greenery, and blessed. This ancient custom survives in Derbyshire, where elaborate well-dressing with floral art is still an established annual event. Love and fertility were the special province of a number of wells. Two Celtic wells offered dominance over one's marriage partner – whoever was the first to drink the water at Ffynnon Gyon, Glamorgan, or St Keyne's Well in Cornwall, would rule the roost. At New Year, and also on l May, the 'cream' or 'flower' of the well – that is, the first water drawn – was credited with magical properties in many areas. It could bestow beauty, luck, a wonderful husband, protection against curses, and even the ability to fly.

Many wells were home to sacred fishes, often trout, which were venerated by Celtic people. The *vesica piscis,* a pointed-oval or almond shape, is a universal symbol for both *yoni* (the tantric term for the vulva) and womb. Celts believed that eating fish encouraged conception – the Irish mythic hero Tuan was eaten by the Queen of Ireland in the form of a fish; she conceived him again, and gave birth to him anew.

♦ ♦ ♦

JOHN THOMAS AND LADY JANE

♦ ♦ ♦

I asked a harder wedding gift than any woman ever asked before from a man in Ireland – the absence of meanness and jealously and fear… If I married a jealous man that would be wrong, too: I never had one man without another waiting in his shadow.

QUEEN MEBDH AND KING AILILL, THE TAIN.

Perhaps the clearest indications that the Celts practised sacred sexual rituals comes from Ireland, where the king traditionally married 'the land', personified by a goddess. In Scotland, a Queen Hermutrude seems to have granted her lovers 'kingship'. Saxo Grammaticus, a

ABOVE *The Main Well, Barlow (Derbyshire, England) decorated with flowers in a tradition which originated with Celtic peoples, honouring their goddess.*

Danish historian, wrote that 'whomsoever she thought worthy of her bed was at once a king, and she yielded her kingdom with herself.'

Pagan customs, which were based on the old Celtic festivals, also support the idea of a sacred marriage between god and goddess. The May Day revels on the old Celtic feast of Beltane (Bright Fire) are brimming over with sexual symbolism and ritual. They were led by a young couple, variously called the May King and Queen, the Lord and Lady, or John Thomas and Lady Jane. The Beltane bonfire was made in a ritualistic fashion by nine men, who were supposed to gather nine kinds of wood. The fire was to be kindled with oak twigs, formerly sacred to the Druids, while nine was a magical Celtic number, sacred to the goddess in many religions.

On May Eve, (30 April, or 11 May in the old calendar) parties of men and women would repair to the woods to 'make green-backs', as it was called in Shakespeare's time. They would return at first light, bearing 'May', that is, hawthorn blossom, or any other flowering greenery. Branches were then placed in people's doorways to bring them luck. They also carried home the inescapably phallic May pole, around which dancing still takes place today. Philip Stubbes offers this description: 'But the chiefest jewel they bring from thence is their May pole, which they bring home with great veneration... This May pole (this stinking Idol rather) is covered all over with flowers and herbs, bound round about with strings from the top to the bottom, and sometimes painted with variable colours... Then fall they to leap and dance about it, as the Heathen people did at the dedication of their idols, wherof this is the perfect pattern, or rather the thing itself.'[105]

Traditionally, the May Games lasted for eight riotous days, and children born 'between the Beltanes' were said to 'have the skill of man and beast', and power over both realms. This superstition is very likely to have once applied to babies conceived during the revels – just as those conceived under similar circumstances in Ancient Greece were said to be children of the gods, since nobody knew for certain who had fathered them.

♦ ♦ ♦

KING ARTHUR AND QUEEN GUINEVERE

♦ ♦ ♦

The Celtic legend of King Arthur, and all the myriad variations of it, seems to be very old, and similarly offers further evidence of sacred sexual beliefs and unions. It was later embroidered upon by the courtly love poets, for whom it was a favourite theme. The adulterous love of Queen Guinevere for Lancelot and Mordred suggests the earlier custom of rulers marrying the goddess. Lancelot and Mordred were both contenders for kingship. Guinevere was Arthur's wife and queen, but in her role of initiatory goddess, it was she who held the true power. Becoming her lover therefore conferred mystical power on her partner – just as the ancient kings of Sumeria could only rule if they underwent the sacred marriage ritual with the high priestess, herself a vehicle of the goddess. The great power of the goddess was offered to male rulers in this way. Without her 'approval', in the form of a sexual encounter, the man was not considered fit to be a leader. Symbolically, this means that a man must make intimate contact with his own instincts and intuition (traditionally regarded as feminine qualities) before taking responsibility for the lives of the others. In this sense she was a sexual object, but she was also much more – a symbol and talisman of Britain and its sovereignty and, on the most profound level, a

representative of the female goddesses of old. In Germany, Guinevere's name was Cunneware, meaning 'female wisdom', a quality she represented in all her roles – as May Queen, as an enchantress, or as the triple goddess of the Celts.

The deeper significance of the romance of King Arthur is only hinted at in medieval poems and stories. A clue is given in the symbolism of names – Arthur means 'heavenly bear', and Uther Pendragon (his father) 'head of the dragon', which is overtly astronomical. The pole-star, the centre of the world, the mill-pole of the universe and the pointer of the earth's axis, is surrounded by the constellations of Ursa Major (the Great Bear) and Draco (the Dragon). Alpha draconis, the head of the

BELOW *This painting is by Brueghel the Younger (1564–1638). The phallic maypole survived all attempts to banish pagan celebration.*

ABOVE *The Zodiac,
showing the symbolic
creatures of each
constellation in the
night sky, by Albrecht
Dürer (Vienna 1515)*

FAR RIGHT *Arthur in
Avalon by Edward Burne-
Jones. The fabled Celtic
king was born of the
goddess and married her in
the form of Guinevere.*

dragon, is the brightest star in Draco. .
The location of the pole-star is identified
by watching the positions of these two
constellations. The myth of Arthur and
his succession therefore describes the
transition of the pole-star from the
dragon to the bear. Even Arthur's origin
is related to the Ninefold Sea-Goddess
who cast him ashore at Merlin's feet.

Arthur was not only born of the
goddess, but also married to the goddess.

His legend therefore is a potent symbol
of the passing of the ages, both in Britain
and the rest of the world. His chivalrous
knights, forever seated at the legendary
Round Table, were imbued with sacred
qualities which were idealized by ordinary men and women in ancient times,
and later in the Middle Ages. Above all,
Arthur and his Queen represent the
mythic quality inherent in us all, and in
our relationships.

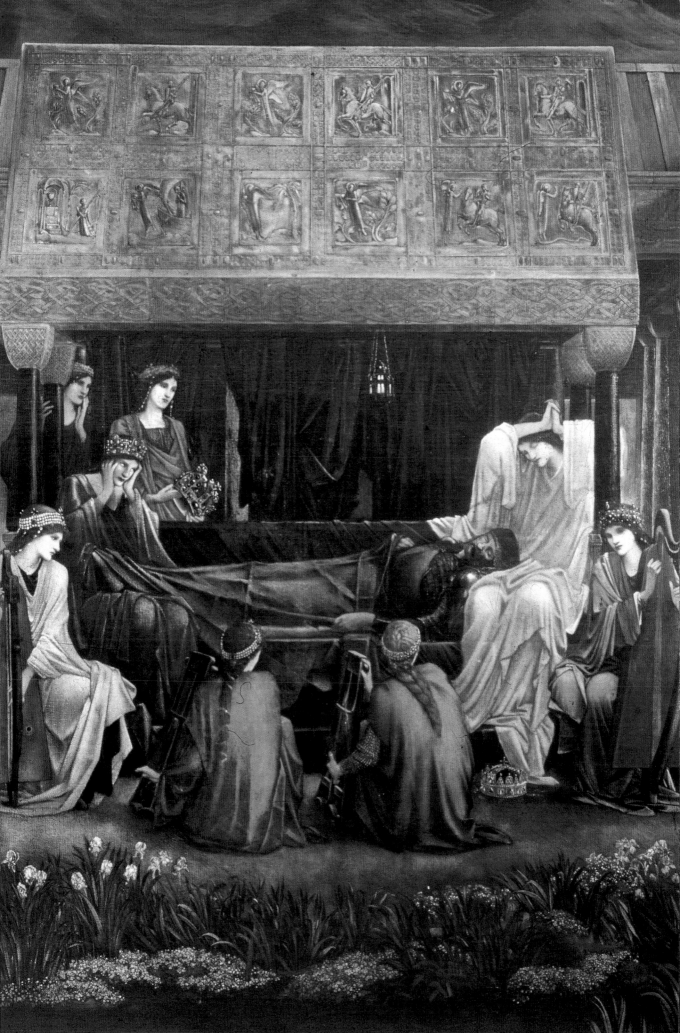

✦ ✦ ✦
THE PAGAN YEAR
✦ ✦ ✦

The pagan year follows a perpetual round of seasonal feasts, many of which are still familiar anniversaries. In northern Europe it drew on both Celtic and Anglo-Saxon traditions, while some of the themes are universal and spring from palaeolithic times. The pagan calendar follows the annual cycle of the goddess as maiden, mother and wise old woman, and the attendant roles played by her lover/consort.

——— F E B R U A R Y ———
Faoilleach – the month of ravaging wolves
Anglo-Saxon: Solmonath – the month of cakes, offered to the goddess
❧ On *1 February*, Celts celebrated the Feast of Imbolc, sacred to St Bride, and at Candlemas (*2 February*) the Feast of the Purification of the Virgin Mary. At this time the goddess, as Maiden, returns from the underworld.

This is the day of Bride
The Queen will come from the Mound
This is the day of Bride
The serpent will come from the hole.

— MARCH —

Gaelic: Earrach Geamraidh, The Winter Spring

Anglo-Saxon: Herthamonath – the month of the goddess Hertha

The month of the spring equinox

— MAY —

Gaelic: Mios Bochuin – the month of swelling

Anglo-Saxon: Thrimilic – the month when cows may be milked three times a day

The Feast of Beltane begins on May Eve, *30th April*, and marks the beginning of summer. The goddess, as May Queen, marries the Green Man, Lord of the Greenwood.

— JUNE —

Gaelic: An t'Og mhios – the young month

Anglo-Saxon: Litha – the month of the midsummer moon

The Summer solstice falls on *21 June*, a time when it was generally thought that supernatural beings were extremely powerful and active.

'Midsummer Eve is counted or called the Witches' Night: and still in many places on St John's Night they make Fires on the hills.'[106]

— AUGUST —

Gaelic: An Lugnasda – the month of the Lammas festival

Anglo-Saxon: Weodmonath – the month of weeds

The Feast of Lammas, or Lugnasadh, when the first sheaf of corn is cut and the Corn King (John Barleycorn) – like all vegetation consorts – must die.

Then they let him lie for a very long time
Till the rain from heaven did fall
The little Sir John sprung up his head
And soon amazed them all.

JOHN BARLEYCORN,
old English folk song

— SEPTEMBER —

Gaelic: An Sultuine – the month of plenty

Anglo-Saxon: Halegmonath – the holy month

Harvest Home festivals were celebrated this month, the last sheaf of standing corn representing the goddess as Corn Mother.

Month of the autumn equinox

— NOVEMBER —

Gaelic: An t-Samhuinn – the month of the Samhain festival

Anglo-Saxon: Blotmonath – the month of blood

The great feast of Samhain, when the goddess descends to the underworld and the spirits of the dead walk, begins on Halloween, *31 October*. Samhain marks the beginning of the Celtic new year.

— DECEMBER —

Gaelic: An Mios marbh – the dead month

Anglo-Saxon: Giuli – the month of Yule

The winter solstice falls on *21 December*, a dark day which had significance as a death and rebirth festival in many cultures. Yule was a time of great sexual licence in ancient times, when people celebrated the lengthening of days and looked forward to the spring.

CHAPTER 12
Fine Medieval Romance

'LADY,' HE ANSWERED, 'SINCE IT PLEASES YOU TO BE SO GRACIOUS, AND TO DOWER SO GRACELESS A KNIGHT WITH YOUR LOVE, THERE IS NAUGHT THAT YOU MAY BID ME DO – RIGHT OR WRONG – THAT I WILL NOT DO TO THE UTMOST OF MY POWER.'[107]

Marie de France, c 1175

Romantic enchantment was born of Celtic myth, wrapped in poetry and cradled in sexual secrets of the most ancient lineage. Its images are full of questing knights, beautiful women and adulterous love affairs – the most popular being the stories of Tristan and Isolde, and Lancelot and Guinevere. These tales, set in a time beyond time, reflect the tension between marital fidelity, the allurements of erotic love, and the irresistible power of passion.

As the medieval Christian Church gained spiritual and temporal power, it sought to impose its beliefs on everyone. Women were often denigrated with great and relentless vigour for they were seen as sinful, seductive beings who wielded the only power the Church truly feared – sexuality. However, fundamental needs and drives have a magical way of surfacing all by themselves, springing up like Dionysus to wreak intoxicating havoc.

Love is a thyng as any spirit free.
Wommen, of kynde, desiren libertee,
And not to be constreyned as a thral;
And so doon men, if I sooth seyen shal.

CHAUCER, THE FRANKLIN'S TALE

During the early medieval period the troubadours, poets, and minnesingers celebrated women, and the love of women, in a way that infuriated the established Church – but which it was unable to suppress. Not all medieval philosophers and churchmen agreed with St Paul, St Jerome, and St Augustine, and they wrestled with the idea that the fall of man was directly linked to the pleasures of the flesh. Albertus Magnus, for example, asserted that it was not pleasure that was evil, but loss of reason – a view also promoted by Thomas Aquinas. Aquinas held that desire and pleasure were not intrinsically wrong, but that evil lay in the submergence of the rational faculty, which occurred during sexual ecstasy.

♦ ♦ ♦
THE GARDEN OF LOVE
♦ ♦ ♦

Indeed, the language and imagery of human love were used by Christian mystics to present allegories of divine love, and the illumination of the eternal soul by the light of heavenly grace. A number of these subtle and thoughtful writers made little distinction between sacred and profane love, while others presented the idea that the spiritual gifts and virtues bestowed by God were the same as those acquired by a lover when he is tested and enlightened by his beloved's grace and acceptance. This is the essence of *amour courtois*. Richard of St Victor, a 12th-century mystic, believed that the spiritual path led towards 'the angelic likeness', and that this was the goal of all spiritual suffering and struggle. He compared the soul's task to the pleasures and torments of love: 'For if he be once admitted to the light-flowing glory of

ABOVE *Lovers are often shown in a garden, symbolizing cultivated nature, a metaphor for courtly love.*

the angelic sublimity… how can we imagine him to press on with secret love-longing, with deep sighs, with unutterable moans!'

This veneration of the divine qualities of human love was explored with great delicacy and feeling by Saint Hildegard of Bingen (1098–1179), one of the most astounding mystics of the Middle Ages. She saw women as the embodiment of a man's love, which in turn had been inspired by God. A living woman thus becomes the mediatrix who leads a man's soul towards illumination through the experience of earthly love, just as the Sumerian temple harlot civilizes and refines the wild man Enkidu, leading him to the city gates to take up a more 'human' existence.

A great visionary, Hildegard wrote of a feminine figure, an unmistakable image of the goddess, who came to her during deep contemplation: 'Then I seemed to see a girl of surpassingly radiant beauty, with such dazzling brightness streaming from her face that I could not behold her fully. She wore a cloak whiter than snow, brighter than stars, her shoes were of pure gold. In her right hand she held sun and moon, and caressed them lovingly. On her breast she had an ivory tablet, on which appeared in shades of sapphire the image of a man. And all creation called this girl sovereign lady. The girl began to speak to the image on her breast: "I was with you in the beginning, in the dawn of your strength and in the brightness of all that is holy, I bore you from the womb before the star of day." And I heard a voice saying to me "The girl whom you behold is Love; she has her dwelling in eternity." '

Hildegard, like all medieval courtly lovers, believed men and women could attain divinity through loving each other, so that 'the whole earth should become like a single garden of love'. And this love was to be whole, a complete expression of union involving both body and soul for, as she wrote, 'It is the power of eternity itself that has created physical union and decreed that two human beings should become physically one.'

♦ ♦ ♦

THE KNIGHT AND THE LADY

♦ ♦ ♦

In thin array after a pleasant guise
When her loose gown
*   from her shoulders did fall,*
And she caught me in her arms
*   long and small*
Therewithal sweetly did me kiss
And softly said, 'Dear heart,
*   how like you this?'*
It was no dream; I lay broad waking.
                         SIR THOMAS WYATT[108]

The world of courtly love, chivalry and homage to women – both living and divine – developed between the 10th and 14th centuries. Crusaders returning from the East, brought fresh life to the dour and dreary world that was emerging from the Dark Ages. As trade routes

ABOVE *Illustration from the Roman de la Rose*
(1487–95) showing the lover and Dame Oyeuse

ABOVE *A picture that accompanied some of the poems of Christine de Pisan, an early feminist. Much courtly love poetry was composed by women.*

The union of erotic and spiritual impulses, the naming and personification of feelings, and the recognition of feminine grace and wisdom found expression here. Powerful noblewomen, such as Eleanor of Aquitaine, became patrons to these poets – and often provided them with raw material for their tales of courtly love.

Chrétien de Troyes, one of the outstanding figures of the 12th century, wrote his romantic tale 'Lancelot and Guinevere' at the behest of the Countess of Champagne who was a great authority on all aspects of courtly love. The Countess supplied the poet with the plot and suggested how it should be presented: Lancelot submits to his Queen completely, and is rewarded by admission into her chamber, where he worships her, genuflecting before leaving his goddess-like beloved.

opened up, vivid silks, satins, exotic spices and jewels flowed from Spain, Turkey and the Arab world. Luxury, sensuality and elegance prevailed in the courts and amongst the nobility – and found expression in the chansons, lays, ballads and romances carried by the troubadours from one castle to the next.

These verses form a large body of literature, much of it allegorical – for, like alchemy, another medieval sub-culture, it hid the sexual knowledge of the East.

Marie de France, who was probably associated with Eleanor of Aquitaine and Henry II, was a prolific and gifted writer of the same period. Her stories are concerned with a range of erotic themes, often emphasizing a woman's desire to choose her lovers, and even to have more than one at the same time. The heroine of the 'Lay of the Dolorous

Knight', for example, has four. It is women who make the sexual advances to men, offering love in exchange for happiness and transformation.

Much of the courtly love poetry composed by female troubadours expressed the poignancy of fleeting moments with a lover, and the delights of passion. Tibors, a 12th-century Provençal noblewoman, told her lover … 'I've never been without desire since it pleased you that I have you as my courtly lover.' Another, Beatriz de Diaz,

longed for a past lover whom she had loved 'to excess':

*How I'd long to hold him pressed
naked in my arms one night –
if I could be his pillow once,
would he not know the height of bliss…
I am giving my heart, my love
my mind, my life, my eyes*[109]

BELOW *Lancelot and Guinevere, whose adulterous love was celebrated by many poets and singers of this period*

ABOVE *Troubadours depicted on an ivory plaque, 1325*

RIGHT *St John and the Great Harlot seated on the waters*

♦ ♦ ♦

TANTRIC TRISTAN

♦ ♦ ♦

The writer and novelist C S Lewis (1898–1963) has suggested that the many magical figures found in courtly love poetry, such as Amor, Jalousie and Pite, are the gods and goddesses of old. The philosophical poets of the school of Chartres (12th century) celebrated and deified nature as a female figure, a notion developed and expanded upon by the poets and artists who were involved with the movement. Certainly, the old order of things had flourished for so many thousands of years that it could not be utterly forgotten, and the more abstract God became, the more people longed for the presence of the divine feminine to comfort them, seeking for ways to incorporate her into the mythology of the Church.

It seems probable that some Crusaders brought back more esoteric secrets from the East, secrets which had their origin in the tantric skill of *maithuna*, or withholding male orgasm. We know that courtly love was more than just a concept – knights and troubadours did actually make love to their chosen ladies. The novelist Lindsay Clarke refers to

RIGHT *Tristan and Iseult, whose tragedy was a favourite theme in courtly love poetry*

ABOVE *Winged hearts, symbolizing romantic
courtship, flit about two young women in a garden*

courtly love poetry as 'Tantric scripts of the West'.[110] Another writer, Edward C Whitmont, suggests that possibly '…it constituted a temporary surfacing of secret religio-erotic cult practices in the service of the Goddess.'[111]

In the cult of courtly love, the woman, like a tantric Shakti, is sexually experienced and uninhibited. She initiates and instructs her lover in the ways of mutual pleasure. He, meanwhile, 'must be able at once to contain himself – for it would be unseemly to allow his sexual impatience to show… '

The couple's first night together, according to several sources, was devoted to a ritual preparation for the act of penetration, using caresses and kisses to enhance and contain instinctual desire on the part of the man, while increasing and intensifying his partner's pleasure. Sexual restraint was also required once penetration had taken place. 'A true lover must seek the interest of his beloved a hundred times more than his own,' said one poet, while others referred to a technique called *drudaria* or *druerie*, which 'can only have been a Western version of Tantric *maithuna*, the sacrament of coitus reservatus'.[112] Tristan, doomed lover of Isolde, provides another intriguing clue when he changes his name to Tantris, offering this secret to

his lover. The cult of courtly love sought to refine and transform its participants, to retrieve the feminine from the dark place where it had languished during the Dark Ages and, above all, to celebrate the joy of love in all its fullness.

Whoever says that Love is sin,
Let him consider first and well:
Right many virtues lodge therein
With which we all, by rights, should dwell.

WALTHER VON DER VOGELWEIDE,
MINNESINGER (C 1170–1230)

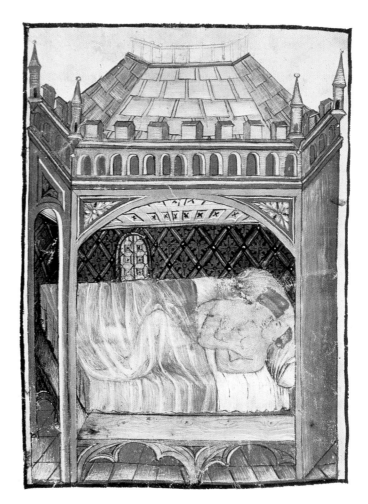

CHAPTER 13

The Alchemical Wedding

ABOVE *The first stage of the alchemical work: Melanosis or blackening*

ABOVE *The second stage of the alchemical work: Leucosis, or whitening*

FAR RIGHT *From the 'Emerald Tablet' of Janitor Pansophus, 1677. The vivid symbolism depicts the alchemical maxim, 'As above, so below', which also pervades other philosophies such as astrology and tarot.*

THE ALCHEMISTS WERE PIONEERS, PEOPLE OPEN TO THE WORLDS WITHIN, WHO PROJECTED THEIR INNER PERCEPTIONS ONTO OUTER SYMBOLS AND THUS FOUND A UNIVERSAL LANGUAGE, TRANSCENDING WORDS, FOR COMMUNICATING THEIR EXPERIENCES OF THE SOUL'S ARCHITECTURE AND DYNAMICS.[113]

Mysterious and richly symbolic, the intricate subculture of alchemy flourished for centuries. Between the 13th and 18th centuries a great body of art and literature was created by alchemists which simultaneously revealed and concealed many esoteric secrets. The work of the alchemists was both mystical and scientific (their experiments in search of 'gold' led to the development of chemistry as we know it), but the reverence with which they regarded their labours, the constantly stressed need for prayer, and their emphasis on secrecy and suffering suggest that there was more to their alchemy than a cursory examination of their writings might reveal.

The great and mystical psychologist, Carl Jung, spent many years immersed in the study of alchemical texts. He perceived them as an allegory of man's quest for wholeness and spiritual development, and observed that the standard Christian teachings of the time were 'not the last answer to the manifold enigmas of man and his soul'. The alchemists sensed the rhythms of the past and the presence of the goddess, and they were aware that 'a vast unknown Nature, disregarded by the eternal verities of the Church, was imperiously demanding recognition and acceptance'.[114]

From any point of view, alchemy involved transmutation. It began with the primal chaos surrounding the prima materia, or first matter, from which the lapis – the ultimate goal of the work, the philosopher's stone – was extracted throughout numerous stages. Many of these stages were characterized by their sexual symbolism: the bisexual hermaphrodite appears as a central figure, while the coniunctio, or sacred marriage, symbolized the most important operation. It is hard to doubt that alchemical teachings concealed magical sexual secrets that were closely allied to tantric knowledge. Because of its complexity and diversity, alchemy certainly cloaked other mysteries in poetic allegory which only the mind of an initiate would be able to penetrate.

The prima materia with which alchemists began their work was found in many things, some of them anciently symbolic of the feminine – for example, water, May dew, the moon, chaos, sea, blood, earth, mother, and even Venus. The shining crown of their search was often personified in the divine feminine form of Sapientia or Sophia, goddess of wisdom, and Siren of the Philosophers. It also appeared in the form of the 'Glorious Child', or *filius philosophorum* – symbolic of the red elixir of life, the precious gold of enlightenment. Many texts refer to the alchemist and his 'mystic sister', with whom he collects the dew and works in the laboratory. She, too, is enjoined to secrecy as they heat and cool, wash and separate the 'substances' in the womb-shaped vessel so characteristic of alchemical imagery.

ABOVE *The third stage of the alchemical work: Xanthosis, or yellowing*

ABOVE *An androgynous figure, metaphor for the union of male and female energies*

FAR RIGHT *An alchemist encounters the spirit of earth, symbolizing the beginning of the alchemical adventure.*

♦ ♦ ♦

THE WATERS OF VENUS

♦ ♦ ♦

The union between male and female, king and queen, sun and moon, is fundamental to all alchemical works, and appears at several stages of the *opus alchymicum* where it is linked with the stages of 'rebirth': for example, the 'first coniunctio' is followed by the nigredo, a stage of black putrefaction often compared with deep depression. The fourth coupling precedes the recovery of the elixir of life from the confusion surrounding the prima materia.

ABOVE *The fourth stage of the alchemical work: Iosis, or reddening*

RIGHT *The sacred Fountain with Sun and Moon, symbols relating to the male and female sexual energies*

At the commencement of the alchemical adventure – the 'opening of the matrix' – the inexperienced philosopher encounters violent, passionate love. This has many symbols – copulating dogs, a fiery sea, a shower of gold gilding a naked queen – and refers to sexual intercourse which lacks the refinement of control and spiritual awareness. The dawning of knowledge is symbolised as two barrels containing the wine of the Earth Mother. The first, forcefully opened by Eros, contains vitriol. The second barrel, gently approached, yields up the wine of Venus, which says 'Intoxicated by my sap, they lose their lives and plunge into a blood bath and show themselves in very beautiful colours. Everybody may wonder at that, as also at my pleasant smell. But methink I hear a wondrous song – that is Frau Venus as far as I can perceive.'

The magical blending of male and female vital essences is often symbolized in liquid form, as the waters of love or the tantric ocean of bliss. (Alchemy itself is full of references to seas, fountains,

milk, blood and ritual baths.) So, awash with alchemical liquids, the mystic couple literally and symbolically 'drown' in the unconscious moment of orgasm, the 'little death' of all worldly concerns which transcends all man-made boundaries and dualities. The 'Rosarium' from the 17th-century *Crowne of Nature* contains this epigram:

*There are two fountains
springing with great power,
The one water is hot and belongs
to the boy; The other water is cold
and is called the virgin's fountain.
Unite the one with the other,
that the two waters may be one:
This stream will possess the forces
of each of them, mixed together,
Just as the fountain of
Jupiter Hammon is simultaneously
hot and cold.*

FAR RIGHT *King Sol and Queen Luna, representing active and receptive, are favourite alchemical figures, each needing the other for balance and transformation.*

The two vital streams of physical and etheric energy are characterized by the colours red and white – menstrual blood and semen, active and receptive, hot and cold, moist and dry – which must be balanced and united to achieve perfection. A five-petalled red and white rose, the Flower of the Alchemists, is often used to signify this mystery which blooms at the heart of the mystical rose garden – a familiar habitation of goddesses, and also the flower of the Virgin Mary. The Red King, redeemed by the White Queen – as the fiery Sol is dissolved by the dark, fertile moisture of Luna – is a persistent alchemical allegory of union and rebirth.

> *White-skinned lady, lovingly*
> *joined to her ruddy-limbed husband,*
> *Wrapped in each other's arms in the bliss*
> *of connubial union, Merge and dissolve as*
> *they come to the goal of perfection:*
> *They that were two are made one, as*
> *though of one body.*[115]

Another universal image, the Tree of Life, is also a recurring alchemical motif. Sometimes it is inverted, with its branches penetrating the earth; in other images the tree is the god Mercurius – the mediating spirit of alchemy – or Adam's phallus in the Garden of Eden. This last symbol shows Adam pierced by the arrow of love, while the tree springs up from his lap, laden with apples. One

ABOVE *The Tree of Life, often identified with sacred knowledge and masculine potency*

alchemist, Pseudo-Aristotle, exhorted his students to: 'Gather the fruits, for the fruit of this tree led us into the darkness and through the darkness.'

It was believed that the tree's sap had magical regenerative properties, and that whoever ate of its fruit would never go hungry. Some philosophers said that its sap was like blood. It was also described as a 'golden tree with seven branches', each putting forth blossoms. It is probable that these seven branches had astrological significance, representing the seven planets of ancient astrology which lent their names to many alchemical substances, figures and processes. These golden branches also offer another irresistible correspondence with tantric teaching, for there are seven major chakras, or energy vortices, in the body, commencing with the muladhara chakra at the base of the spine which is visualized as red, and proceeding to the sahasrara chakra at the crown, visualized as pure white light. It is this union of soul and spirit, the sense of an immanent divinity, which is the ecstatic goal of alchemy and, indeed, all sacred mysteries.

> *The things that are in the realms above*
> *Are also in the realms beneath.*
> *What Heaven shows is often found*
> *   on earth.*
> *Fire and flowing water are contraries,*
> *Happy thou if thou canst unite them.*[116]

FAR RIGHT *The fifth key from the Keys of Basil Valentine shows Venus, goddess of love, with the lion.*

RIGHT *The double dragon between Sun and Moon, symbolizing sexual energies which must be transformed during the course of alchemical work*

CHAPTER 14

Aztec Feathered Serpent Rising

ABOVE *The Goddess
Coatlicue (Aztec,
15th century)*

FAR RIGHT
*Hermaphroditic Aztec
god/dess Ometecuhtli
(Aztec, Mexico stone
figure). Ometecuhtli was
both male and female and
the supreme creative deity
in the Aztec pantheon.
This seated figure shows
him/her in the form of
Tonacatecuhtli, the Lord of
Fate. On the headdress is
the mask of the Star
Dragon, a sign of the
Milky Way.*

BELOW *Quetzalcoatl, the
Plumed Serpent (Aztec,
15th century)*

YOU ARE IN HEAVEN:
YOU UPHOLD THE MOUNTAIN.
THE PLANE OF EARTH IS IN
YOUR HANDS.
AWAITED, YOU ARE ALWAYS
EVERYWHERE.
YOU ARE PRAYED TO: YOU ARE
INVOKED.[117]

The seemingly different culture that emerged among the Aztecs in Central America has fundamental traces in common with the kundalini mythology of the far East. The above hymn to the Ometecuhtli Omecihuatl praises the transcendent one, the creator of the world, who is also called the 'Lord-Lady of Duality', like Vishnu. Shown as two opposing serpent heads which are simultaneously one, he/she is the culmination of the 13 heavens, identifying him/her with the realm of the lunar goddess (there are 13 lunar cycles in the year). This supreme being is both transcendent and engaged in the world, powerful at the centre and capable of destruction.

Coatlicue, the Lady of the Serpent Skirt, the all-powerful Aztec goddess/mother of the universe, prepares for the creation of a new prehistoric world age. She is shown with a skull (a common Tibetan Buddhist symbol) between her navel and genitals, symbolizing the ultimate power that generates, produces and consumes all life in the world. She moderates between the heavenly world above and the hellish underworld below by bestowing life and thriving on death. She is a terrifying figure, to whom priests sacrificed victims by cutting out their hearts, but she is also goddess of love and creation.

Following the end of a world age, the resurrected god Quetzalcoatl returns from the domain of the underworld god with a package of broken bones. The Lady of the Serpent Skirt grinds them up, pours them into a clay vessel and entreats Quetzalcoatl to empty his member into it; and with all the other gods and goddess praying for penance, a new people comes into being.[118] Although described in a prosaic way, this integration between female and male certainly turned the tables on male dominance in the outer world.

To the Toltecs and Aztecs, the body of the universal goddess was composed of time and space. Like the Egyptian Nut, she was a sky goddess, wearing her raiment of stars which nightly swallowed up the sun-god Quetzalcoatl and resurrected him every morning. Naturally therefore she was symbolic of the integration of the four directions of the compass and the stars, and of male and female sexual energies. The Toltec myth of resurrection resembles Buddhist, Christian, Chaldean and medieval beliefs in that their god was born of a virgin and was crucified and resurrected.[119]

The mother of Quetzalcoatl was one of three virgins who were visited by the highest god-of-the-gods in the morning light. She was the only one to conceive, but died in giving birth.

From birth, Quetzalcoatl could speak and possessed all understanding, knowledge and wisdom. He was the legendary originator of language, of the arts of life, and of the calendar, reigning in a temple/palace which had rooms radiating in the four cardinal directions, each symbolizing the qualities of the world. He grew old and white, and was loved, venerated and respected by all people.

ABOVE *Quetzalcoatl rises from the jaws of the Feathered Serpent (Aztec green jade, Mexico), just as the Morning Star rises from the earth to herald the new sunrise. He wears a collar symbolic of the sun. This probably commemorates a transit of Venus in 1508.*

ABOVE RIGHT *Mayan Altar of the sun from Palenque, Mexico*

A young god came to the palace one day and presented Quetzalcoatl with a mirror wrapped in a rabbit skin, into which the wise one looked. He saw himself as infirm, sick and of hideous demeanour, and was shocked by what he saw. The young god presented him with a magic potion which, after initially rejecting, Quetzalcoatl drank. He became intoxicated and sent for his sister, Quetzalpetlatl, who also drank of the bowl. They spent the night together in each other's embrace. In the morning, Quetzalcoatl was shamed and realized that he was no longer fit to rule.

Upon burning his temple and disposing of his possessions, he wandered across the plains and over the mountains. After losing a sacred ball game, he aimed and shot his last arrow through the sacred pochotl tree, making a cross, which became his symbol. He continued walking to the place where sea, land and sky meet and sailed away on a raft of serpents, although his heart returned after four days as the morning star, Venus.

The imagery created in many cultures to commemorate this legend takes the form of mandalas which depict

Quetzalcoatl's heart embedded in the square of the goddess of death, in the centre of which are intertwined feathered serpents. This motif is similar to that of Vishnu and his consort overarched by the serpent, and portrays the simultaneous identity of the goddess as both his consort and his death.

The double serpent is also shown as the conduit through which two human figures are disgorged in the south-east as the morning star, which was sacred to love-making. As in the Egyptian genesis, the goddess is also covered with stars and is surrounded by, or composed of, the symbolic elements of the Aztec calendar.

The fabulous culture of Central and South America was highly evolved, but the people lived in a constant state of existential terror concerning what they felt to be the intangible nature of life. This anxiety was expressed in their equal love of female and male, life and death. Ritual sacrifices to the creators and destroyers of life were central to their beliefs, and they ultimately felt that life itself was nothing more than a mask worn on the face of death. For them, the vitality of incarnation through the sexual act led them once again into mortality and an ultimate meeting with the goddess of the underworld.

BELOW Quetzalcoatl the plumed serpent was the god of wind, learning and the priesthood, the master of life, creator and civilizer, patron of every art and inventor of metallurgy to the Aztecs and Toltecs.

CHAPTER 15
Esoteric Sacred Sexuality

Alice A Bailey was an English woman who for many years in the early part of this century telepathically communicated with a Master of the Hierarchy called 'The Tibetan'[120] and wrote numerous books on their contact. This body of work is considered 'esoteric' knowledge which is given to humanity as the New Age comes closer to reality. Unlike other contemporary traditions, these works address the issue of sacred sexuality in our time in an informative and sensible way. Many of The Tibetan's statements about sexuality are very relevant, even though the most recent are already more than 50 years old.

According to The Tibetan, sex is the relationship between matter and spirit, or the lower nature and the higher Self, in common with the Hindu and Buddhist traditions. When elevated to its proper level, its function is to allow humanity to achieve complete union with divinity. Although sex is a physical function, sometimes carried out under the impulse of love, when it is illuminated by soul awareness it becomes a transcendent force for achieving higher consciousness.

The Tibetan believed that sexual force emanates from the physical plane and therefore creates a pull towards energy which is involutionary (returning to the roots) rather than evolutionary (expanding into higher consciousness), which means that on a cosmic level sexuality is regressive rather than progressive. Its sacred function is to bring the lower self into realization, just as its physical function is to bring new and pure bodies into being. Our present attitude to sexuality has its origins in the behaviour of early humanity which, being integral to the physical world,

practised sex as a sinless way to procreate. But as emotions became more developed – and more uncontrollable – sinful attitudes appeared and the sacred function of the sex act became debased into the satisfaction of desire.

Now that humanity is beginning to function primarily upon the mental level characteristic of initiates, it is possible to restore sex to its proper role, with the soul assuming control of the three bodies – the physical, emotional and mental. This implies that it is essential to purify and sublimate the functions of the lower bodies in the service of the higher in order to emanate the most harmonious energies, which in turn have a beneficial effect not only upon an individual, but upon his or her partner.

The profound change in attitude towards sexuality expressed through the above idea makes clear that the positive symbolism of sex has commonly been forgotten today, and the thoughts which replace it are animalistic and perverse. The sacred mystery has been lost, and with it the power of sexuality to uplift, to transcend, and to be a vehicle of true and profound love. Indeed, some people attempt to create a gateway to higher consciousness through the sexual channel alone, trying to find the fusion which they require through their physical level of being. Even with the highest motives in mind, it must be realized that sex represents and symbolizes an inner duality which must itself be transcended. It can therefore never be an end in itself. This transcendence is not achieved physically, but consciously. When this principle becomes common knowledge, it will lead to a new and more reverential attitude between male and female, between races, and between humanity

FAR RIGHT *The Day Dream (1880) by Dante Gabriel Rossetti (1828–1882). The Pre-Raphaelites idealized the female in form and imagination.*

and the earth (Gaia). In many ways a new sexual ecology is needed for the new humanity.[121]

It is clear that sexuality in modern times is a panacea for the loneliness and fear that most people experience in their lives. Indeed, sexuality has become in the minds of many the only force capable of counteracting this existential dilemma.

♦ ♦ ♦

LOVE AND SEX

♦ ♦ ♦

An extremely important question is the relationship between love and sex, which The Tibetan understood as similar ways of saying the same thing, although both have lost their true meaning. Love and sex exemplify the Law of Attraction – on the interpersonal level between sexes, on the intrapersonal level between the individual and the soul, and on the universal level, where it represents a dynamic bringing humanity together with God.

In all the above cases the motivating factor is the karmic influence – it's the thought that counts. The result of all interactions motivated by sexuality is manifestation – whether of a physical being, an emotion, or a relationship. The outcome is always related directly to the attitudes of the partners and the repercussions will be included in their karmic heritage. Just as love is productive, so these sexual attractions always produce results, either positive or negative, according to how the seed is sown. On the highest level, both love and sex generate a profound godlike energy within a person, which is the best possible result of the sexual act. Sex symbolizes this process, even though it is often correlated with the outcome of the process.

When blending sexual energies, it is necessary to fuse the energies from the lower chakras, manifest through the personality, with the energies from the higher chakras, manifest through the Heart, Throat and Brow centres. These transformations can happen in artistic, creative or spiritual ways, but the metaphor activating them is the translation of the lower into the higher, the foundation of sacred sexuality. When lower and higher blend and merge, what emerges from this divine synthesis is pure beauty. And physical sex is the symbol of this profound process.

In the future the transformations which will have the most powerful effects upon humanity will be those in which the higher energies of the human race emerge and become dominant.

RIGHT *Chinese Pa-Kwa symbol, which symbolizes the integration of male and female energies and magically restores the balance between their opposing but reciprocal qualities.*

Afterword

Sacred Sexuality is intended to intrigue and challenge you – and perhaps inspire you to explore the ideas we present in this book. We are writing at a time when the Western world is searching for answers. The structures – political, personal, spiritual and sexual – which served our parents and grandparents are no longer appropriate. Collective confusion prevails as we seek meaning and harmony in our lives. So it must be during any time of revolution, for nothing new can be born without a period of chaos and darkness. Such times are reflected in the ancient creation myths explored here. Indeed, Eros – god of erotic love – was himself born of night and chaos.

The essential aim of all sacred sexual practices is to offer transcendental experience. This is achieved through a conscious submission to passion and ecstasy which fully involves both partners, body and soul. Sacred sexuality embraces all the senses, vivifies the emotions, and engages the spirit. Ultimately, it is something that can be experienced only in a part of the psyche which has no word, logic, dogma or creed.

Modern 'goddess movements' represent a reaching out towards these buried truths, for the goddess or divine feminine has been severely neglected both within and without. Instinctive knowing, intuitive guidance, and receptivity are popularly labelled 'feminine' qualities, belonging to the goddess of a thousand names and cultures. However, we believe that these qualities are the birthright of all human beings, whatever their gender or sexual orientation. Expressing and experiencing ourselves through the love of another is very much a part of life – and for many people life without a relationship with another is meaningless and barren.

In our eagerness to understand the dynamics of relationship, sexuality is often relegated to second place. We study sexual techniques and positions, and forget all about the role of sensuality and instinctive feelings in our everyday lives. As a society, we have put sexual expression in a small box where we hope to contain and control it. We use statistics and manuals to tell us what is 'normal' and what everyone else is doing, as if we are trying to distance ourselves from the mystery of sexual love. But all the research in the world cannot teach us what the ancients once knew and celebrated. Sexuality is both numinous mystery and visceral act, animal and spiritual, lusty and soulful. Within its centre there is no paradox, for it represents the perfect blending of Yin and Yang, active and passive. Sexuality is sacred, because life itself is sacred.

ABOVE *Sleeper II by Caroline Smith. The dormant feminine is arising and will take its rightful place as equal and composite to the masculine in the emerging new world age.*

Notes

Chapter 1

1   James M Robinson, *The Nag Hammadi Library in English*, p 169.
2   Ibid, p 171.
3   The gods wanted to create an empty vessel with no feminine influence, over which they could rule. The soul Eve gave Adam symbolizes the animating, feminine quality within all men.
4   Emma Jung and Marie Louise von Franz, *The Grail Legend*, pp 36–7.

Chapter 2

5   For more about paleolithic people, see Auel, *The Clan of the Cave Bear*, Hodder, London, 1981.
6   Serpent, snake and dragon are often interchangeable terms.
7   Mircea Eliade, *The Sacred and the Profane*, p 48.
8   Heinrich Zimmer, *Myths and Symbols in Indian Art and Civilization*, p 59.
9   Monica Sjöö and Barbara Mor, *The Great Cosmic Mother*, p 57.
10   A T Mann, *Sacred Architecture*, pp 60–9, 79–82.
11   Julius Evola, *The Metaphysics of Sex*, pp 124–6.
12   Penny Slinger and Nik Douglas, *Sexual Secrets*, p 133.
13   Evola, op cit, p 128.
14   The calendar is made by the passage of the sun through the seasons and their equivalent zodiac signs. Calendrical myths express this process through the killing and dismemberment of the dragon, usually into 12 parts. Sometimes the 13th part, as symbolized by the Osiris myth, stands for the five extra intercalary days in the year (12 x 30 + 5 = 365).
15   Sjöö and Moor, op cit, p 106.

Chapter 3

16   Nancy Qualls-Corbett, *The Sacred Prostitute*, p 40
17   Lucretius (94–55 BC), *The Nature of the Universe*.
18   Simone de Beauvoir, *The Second Sex*, Pan, London, 1988.
19   W Carew Hazlitt, *Faiths and Folklore of the British Isles*, Benjamin Blom Inc, New York, 1965.
20   Nickie Roberts, *Whores in History*, p 64
21   Philip Stubbes, *The Anatomy of Abuses*.

Chapter 4

22   Ishtar/Inanna identified herself (through her myths) as a prostitute, and was worshipped as such in Babylon for thousands of years. The Whore of Babylon was one of her titles, although the word 'whore' did not then carry the pejorative sense it acquired later. The myth of Ishtar was developed by Hebrew priests who were well aware of her worship. Later, it seems, knowledge was lost and the Sumerian/Babylonian culture forgotten by later interpreters of the old texts, who took Whore of Babylon to mean Rome, another rather sexual culture.
23   Akkadian hymn of praise, quoted in Barbara Walker, *The Woman's Encyclopedia of Myths and Secrets*, p 452.
24   Anne Baring and Jules Cashford, *The Myth of the Goddess*, p 197.
25   *The Epic of Gilgamesh* was a Sumerian poem, written down in about 2000 BC. It is one of the earliest written poems in existence today.
26   Diane Wolkstein and Samuel Noah Kramer, *Innana, Queen of Heaven and Earth: Her Stories and Hymns from Sumer*, Harper Collins, London, 1983, p 36. Quoted in Baring and Cashford, p 187.
27   Reay Tannahill, *Sex in History*, p 50.
28   Wendy Buonaventura, *Belly Dancing*, Virago Press, London, 1983, p 23.
29   Herodotus, *The Histories* (3 BC), quoted in Qualls-Corbett, op cit, p 34.
30   Samuel Kramer, *History Begins at Sumer*, Thames & Hudson, London, 1958. p 286.
31   Samuel Kramer, *The Sacred Marriage Rite*, Indiana University Press, 1969, p 63.

Chapter 5

32   Robert Bauval and Adrian Gilbert, *The Orion Mystery*, p 92.
33   Kart Sethe, *Die Altaegyptischen Pyramidentexte*, Leipzig, 1908–22.
34   Sjöö and Mor, op cit, p 58.
35   R A Schwaller de Lubicz (1887–1961) was a controversial French philosopher, hermetist and Egyptologist.
36   Schwaller de Lubicz, *Symbol and Symbolic*, p 8.
37   John Anthony West, *Serpent in the Sky*, pp 153–4.
38   Schwaller de Lubicz, *Sacred Science*, p 187.
39   Ibid, p 187.
40   Egyptian and other mythologies refer to the primordial ocean as existing before anything else, and that it was without light, endless, without boundaries or direction – in short, empty space.
41   Ibid, p 190.
42   Ibid, p 192.
43   Gay Robins, *Women in Ancient Egypt*, p 17.
44   *Symbol and Symbolic*, p 151.
45   Ibid, p 27.
46   Robins, op cit, pp 189–90.
47   Walker, op cit, p 821.

Chapter 6

48   This myth was originally written with 'self' as 'he'. Paraphrased from Robert O Ballou (ed.), *The Bible of the World* p 38.
49   Zimmer, op cit, pp 61–8.
50   Evola, op cit, p 122.
51   Ibid, p 67.
52   Zimmer, op cit, p 190.
53   Ibid, p 191.
54   Ibid, p 191.
55   Brhadaranyake Upanishad 4.3, 21–22, translated by Hume, in Zimmer, *Philosophies of India*, p 371.
56   According to the Sänkhya and yoga philosophies, the life-monad, variously called purusha, 'man', ätman or 'self', is the living entity which animates, but which is also concealed behind and within human life, cf Zimmer, *Philosophies of India*, p 285.
57   Here 'Aryan' means 'civilized', rather than referring to a particular race: Mark Balfour, *The Sign of the Serpent*, p 4.
58   Zimmer, *Philosophies of India*, pp 363–4.
59   Aryan, Nirvanamanjari, quoted in Zimmer, *Philosophies of India*, p 463.
60   'Yoga', meaning 'yoke' connecting the individual to the One.
61   See Jung's essay 'On Psychic Energy' in *The Structure and Dynamics of the Psyche*, pp 3–67.
62   Wilhelm Reich (1897–1957) was a German psychotherapist who developed radical theories on the relationship between sexuality, orgasm and the psychological functioning. See his *Theory of the Orgasm*, Pandora, London, 1992.
63   David V Tansley, *Subtle Body*, p 26.
64   Ibid, p 26.

65   For a more complete treatment of the components of tantric sexuality, see Slinger and Douglas, op cit.
66   Ibid, p 151.

Chapter 7

67   'Synchronicity' was a term created by the psychologist C G Jung, meaning 'an acausal connecting principle', a peculiar interdependence of objective events among themselves as well as subjective states of the observer. See Jung's foreword to the *I Ching*, translated by Richard Wilhelm, p xiv.
68   Ibid, pp 298–9.
69   Ibid, p 298.
70   Lao Tzu, *Tao Te Ching*, translated by Richard Wilhelm, p 27.
71   Mantak Chia, *Taoist Secrets of Love: Cultivating Male Sexual Energy*, pp xvii et al. Together with *Healing Love Through the Tao: Cultivating Female Sexual Energy*, these two books are probably the best technical manuals for developing Taoist sexual techniques. Master Chia has studied with Taoist and Buddhist masters and teaches through numerous centres in the United States and Europe.
72   Ibid, p xvii.
73   Daniel Reid, *The Tao of Health, Sex and Longevity*, pp 272–4.
74   Ibid, p 276.
75   See Chia, *Healing Love Through the Tao: Cultivating Female Sexual Energy*.
76   Ibid, pp 40–2.
77   Sukie Colegrave, *The Spirit of the Valley: Androgyny and Chinese Thought*, pp 182–4.

Chapter 8

78   Part of a Homeric Hymn to Gaia, translated by Jules Cashford, *The Myth of the Goddess*, p 303. Used by permission of Jules Cashford.
79   Aeschylus, *Danaides*, Baring and Cashford, op cit, p 363.
80   Indra Sinha, *Tantra, the Search for Ecstasy*, p 41.
81   Roberto Calasso, *The Marriage of Cadmus and Harmony*, p 44.

82   Ibid, p 45
83   Quoted in Sinha, op cit, p 47.

Chapter 9

84   *Encyclopaedia of World Mythology*, ed. Rex Warner.
85   Homeric hymn, translated by J Cashford in Harvest, Vol 35, 1989–90, p 209. *Harvest* is a periodical with private circulation amongst Jungian analysts.
86   Ovid, Fasti, 5, lines 201–15.
87   Translated by J P Postgate, Loeb Classical Library, quoted in *The Bedside Book*, Gollancz, c1932.
88   Ovid, op cit.
89   Ibid.
90   Barbara G Walker is a prominent American researcher and writer, particularly in the field of women's studies.

Chapter 10

91   'The Thunder, Perfect Mind', *The Nag Hammadi Library in English*, p 272.
92   Walker, op cit, p 947.
93   From Marina Warner, *Beast to the Blonde*, Chatto & Windus, London, 1994, p 125.
94   'Gnostic Gospel of Philip', *The Nag Hammadi Library in English*, p 138.

Chapter 11

95   *The Feminist Companion to Mythology*, Pandora, London, 1992. p 120.
96   Quoted in Maureen Duffy, *The Erotic World of Faery*.
97   Anonymous Gaelic poem, quoted in Eric Ericson, *The World, The Flesh and The Devil*.
98   Joan Halifax, *Shaman, The Wounded Healer*, Thames & Hudson, London, 1982.
99   Duffy, op cit, p 105.
100 P H Ditchfield, *Old English Customs Extant at the Present Time: An Account of Local Observance, Festival Customs, and Ancient Ceremonies, Yet Surviving in Great Britain*, George Redway, London, 1896.
101 Strabo (c64 BC–c22 AD), Greek geographer and traveller.
102 Doreen Valiente, *Natural Magic*, Hale, 1975. Doreen Valiente is a practising witch and author of a number of books on Wicca.
103 John Michell, *The Earth Spirit*, p 76.
104 Quoted in Duffy, op cit, p 87.
105 Stubbes, op cit.
106 John Aubrey, *Remains of Gentilism*, 1688.

Chapter 12

107 Marie de France, c1175, translated by Eugene Mason, J M Dent, London, 1964.
108 Quoted in Duffy, op cit, p 39.
109 Poem from *An Anthology of the Provençal Troubadours*, Raymond Hill and Thomas G Burgin (eds), 1941, p 96.
110 Lindsay Clarke, *Alice's Masque*, Picador, 1994.
111 Edward C Whitmont, *The Return of the Goddess*, Arkana, 1987, p 175.
112 Walker, op cit, p 862.

Chapter 13

113 Dr Irene Gad, *Tarot and Individuation*, p 111.
114 C G Jung, *Psychology and Alchemy*, p 196.
115 'The Crowne of Nature', quoted in Johannes Fabricius, Alchemy, p 81.
116 *The Twelve Keys of Basil Valentine*, Germany, 1599.

Chapter 14

117 Joseph Campbell, *The Mythic Image*, p 157.
118 Ibid, p 156.
119 Ibid, pp 172–81.

Chapter 15

120 The Master Djwhal Khul did not reveal his identity, but lived in a physical body near the borders of Tibet. He transmitted *The Secret Doctrine* and *Isis Unveiled* to Madame Blavatsky, the founder of the Theosophical Society in England in 1875.
121 Alice Bailey, *Esoteric Astrology*, Lucis Trust, New York, 1951, p 385.

PICTURE CREDITS   **Ancient Art and Architecture Collection**: pp. 15-16, 17, 20, 21TL, 24TL, 34, 35TL, 43BR, 48, 57 TL &BR, 62, 63TR, 66BL, 77, 87R, 89TR, 97, 98TL, 99, 102, 107, 108-9, 109T, 126, 127, 128, 129, 133, 136-7, 151, 169TL, 178, 180; **Bridgeman Art Library**: pp. 9, 11, 13, 19, 22, 23, 26-7, 29, 30, 31, 33, 35BR, 37, 39, 48-9, 51, 61, 66 TL, 70, 76, 94, 100-1, 104-5, 110, 114-5, 116-7, 118, 120, 122, 124, 131, 132, 134, 135R, 138-9, 140, 142-3, 144, 147, 150, 155, 157, 162-3, 164-5, 166, 167, 168, 169BR, 173, 181, 183, 185; **Collections/Brian Shuel**: p. 154; **C M Dixon**: pp. 18, 21, 24B, 41, 46, 64, 67B, 89TR, 102, 109B, 119, 148TL; **Fine Art Photographic Library**: pp. 28, 53, 161, 166T; **Giraudon/Bridgeman Art Library**: pp. 32, 55; **Gisbert Bauer**: p. 76; **The Hutchinson Library**: pp. 65, 78, 107BR; **Images Colour Library Ltd**: pp. 79, 82TL, 84TL & BL, 85, 91, 93, 171, 172174-5, 176BR, 177; **Index/Bridgeman Art Library**: p. 7; **Lauros-Giraudon/Bridgeman Art Library**: pp. 44, 47, 112-3; **Mary Evans Picture Library**: pp. 36TL, 152, 176TL; **Ronald Sheridan**: pp. 42TL, 45, 89B; Courtesy of the artist, **Caroline Smith**: pp. 12, 25, 186; **Werner Foreman Archive**: pp. 40, 54, 56, 59, 63, 68; **Werner Foreman Archive/Haiphang Museum, Vietnam**: p. 81; **Werner Foreman Archive/Museum für Völkerkunde, Basel**: p. 179; **Werner Foreman Archive/National Museum, Copenhagen**: pp. 148BL, 149; **Werner Foreman Archive/Philip Goldman Collection**: pp. 67TR, 74TL; **Werner Foreman Archive/Private Collection**: pp. 69,72-3, 83BR.

Bibliography

BAILEY, ALICE A, and TIBETAN MASTER DJWHAL KHUL, *A Compilation on Sex*, Lucis Trust, New York, 1984

BALFOUR, MARK, *The Sign of the Serpent*, Prism, Bridport, 1990

BALLOU, ROBERT O, (ed), *The Bible of the World*, Kegan Paul Trench Trubner, London, 1940

BARING, ANNE, and CASHFORD, JULES, *The Myth of the Goddess*, Penguin Books, 1993

BAUVAL, ROBERT and GILBERT, ADRIAN, *The Orion Mystery*, William Heinemann, London, 1994

BYRON, JOHN, *Portrait of a Chinese Paradise: Erotica and Sexual Customs of the Late Qing Period*, Quartet Books, London, 1987

CALASSO, ROBERTO, *The Marriage of Cadmus and Harmony*, Vintage, London, 1994

CAMPBELL, JOSEPH, *The Mythic Image*, Princeton, 1974

CAMPHAUSEN, RUFUS, *The Encyclopedia of Erotic Wisdom*, Inner Tradition, New York, 1990

CHIA, MANTAK and CHIA, MANEEWAN, *Healing Love Through the Tao: Cultivating Female Sexual Energy*, Healing Tao Books, Huntington, 1986

— and WINN, MICHAEL, *Taoist Secrets of Love:Cultivating Male Sexual Energy*, Aurora Press, New York, 1984

COLEGRAVE, SUKIE, *The Spirit of the Valley: Androgyny and Chinese Thought*, Virago, London, 1979.

DUFFY, MAUREEN, *The Erotic World of Faery*, Hodder & Stoughton, London, 1972

ELIADE, MIRCEA, *From Primitives to Zen*, Collins, London, 1967

— *The Sacred and the Profane*, trans. Willard Trask, Harcourt Brace & World, San Diego, 1959

ERICSON, ERIC, *The World, The Flesh and The Devil*, New English Library, London, 1981

EVOLA, JULIUS, *The Metaphysics of Sex*, East-West Publications, London, 1983

FABRICIUS, JOHANNES, *Alchemy*, Rosenkilde & Bagger, Copenhagen, 1976

FRAZER, JAMES G, *The Golden Bough: A Study of Magic and Religion*, Macmillan, London, 1950

GAD, DR IRENE, *Tarot and Individuation*, Nicholas-Hays Inc, York Beach, Maine, 1994

HAICH, ELISABETH, *Sexual Energy and Yoga*, trans. D Q Stephenson, Aurora Press, New York, 1982

HUMANA, C and WANG WU, *The Chinese Way of Love*, Hong Kong, 1982

JOHARI, HARISH, *Tools for Tantra*, Destiny Books, Vermont, 1986

JORDAN, MICHAEL, *Myths of the World*, Kyle Cathie, London, 1993

JUNG, C G, *Alchemical Studies*, trans. R F C Hull, Routledge & Kegan Paul, London, 1973

— *Psychology and Alchemy*, trans. R F C Hull, Routledge & Kegan Paul, London, 1974

— *The Structure and Dynamics of the Psyche*, trans. R F C Hull, Routledge & Kegan Paul, London, 1960

JUNG, EMMA, and VON FRANZ, MARIE LOUISE, trans. Andrea Dykes, *The Grail Legend*, G P Puttnams, New York, 1970

KHANNA, MADHU, *Yantra: The Tantric Symbol of Cosmic Unity*, Thames & Hudson, London, 1979

LARSEN, CYNTHIA and SHANNON, PAUL, *The Synchronicity Guidebook*, Amethyst Publishing, Nellysford, 1994

LARSEN, STEPHEN, *The Mythic Imagination*, Bantam, New York, 1990

LAO TZU, *Tao Te Ching*, trans. Richard Wilhelm, Arkana, London, 1985

MANN, A T, *Sacred Architecture*, Element, Shaftesbury, 1993

MICHELL, JOHN, *The Earth Spirit*, Thames & Hudson, London, 1988

MOOKERJEE, AJIT and MADHU KHANNA, *Tantra*, trans. Niels Brunse, Forlaget Rhodos, Svendborg, 1977

QUALLS-CORBETT, NANCY, *The Sacred Prostitute*, Inner City Books, Toronto 1988

RAWSON, PHILIP, *The Art of Tantra*, Thames & Hudson, London, 1978

— *The Indian Cult of Ecstasy*, Thames & Hudson, London, 1973

REID, DANIEL, *The Tao of Health, Sex and Longevity*, Simon & Schuster, London, 1989

ROBERTS, JANE, *The Nature of the Psyche: Its Human Expression*, A Seth Book, Prentice Hall, New York, 1979

ROBERTS, NICKIE, *Whores in History*, Grafton, London, 1993

ROBINS, GAY, *Women in Ancient Egypt*, British Museum Press, London, 1993

ROBINSON, JAMES M, (Director), *The Nag Hammadi Library in English*, E J Brill, Leiden, 1977

SCHWALLER DE LUBICZ, R A, *Sacred Science*, trans. André and Goldian VandenBroeck, Inner Traditions, New York, 1982

— *Symbol and Symbolic*, trans. Robert Lawlor, Autumn Press, Brookline, 1978

— *The Temple in Man*, trans. Robert and Deborah Lawlor, Autumn Press, Brookline, 1977

SINHA, INDRA, *Tantra, the Search for Ecstasy*, Hamlyn, London, 1993

SKINNER, STEPHEN, *The Living Earth Manual of Feng-Shui: Chinese Geomancy*, Routledge & Kegan Paul, London, 1982

SLINGER, PENNY, and DOUGLAS, NIK, *Sexual Secrets*, Destiny Books, Rochester, 1979

SJÖÖ, MONICA, and MOR, BARBARA, *The Great Cosmic Mother*, Harper & Row, San Francisco and New York, 1975

STEIN, DIANE, *The Kwan Yin Book of Changes*, Llewellyn, St Paul, 1986

STUBBES, PHILIP, *The Anatomy of Abuses*, London, 1586

TANNAHILL, REAY, *Sex in History*, London, 1980

TANSLEY, DAVID V, *Chakras, Rays and Radionics*, C W Daniel, Saffron Walden, 1984

— *Subtle Body*, Thames & Hudson, London, 1977

VAN GULIK, R H, *Sexual Life in Ancient China*, Leiden, 1961

WALKER, BARBARA G, *The Woman's Encyclopedia of Myths and Secrets*, Harper & Row, San Francisco, 1983

WARNER, REX, (ed), *Encyclopaedia of World Mythology*, BPC Publishing, London, 1975

WEST, JOHN ANTHONY, *Serpent in the Sky*, Harper & Row, New York, 1979

WILHELM, RICHARD, (trans), *I Ching, The Book of Changes*, foreword by C G Jung, Bollingen Series XIX, Princeton, 1950

ZIMMER, HEINRICH, *Myths and Symbols in Indian Art and Civilization*, ed Joseph Campbell, Bollingen, Washington, 1946

— *Philosophies of India*, ed Joseph Campbell, Meridian Books, New York, 1956.

ADAM – The first created being according to the Bible, but also a symbol of the masculine principle.

ANUBIS – The Egyptian jackal god, present at the judgement of souls.

ASTROLOGICAL GREAT YEAR – The movement of the spring equinox point, describing a conical ellipse around the north pole star, takes about 25,000 years, or approximately 2,000 years per sign backwards through the zodiac.

ĀTMAN – The eternal spiritual entity, the universal Self.

ATUM – Egyptian sun god, symbolic of knowledge.

BEAST OF PARADISE – The serpent or snake entwining the Tree of Good and Evil in the Biblical Garden of Eden.

CADUCEUS – The staff of the Greek god Hermes (Roman Mercury), entwined by two snakes and surmounted by two wings or a helmet. It symbolizes wisdom and power.

CHAKRAS – The seven or more energy centres in the human body located near the spinal column, the function of which is to transmit and balance life force.

CHAOS – An early biblical description of the universe when it was pure energy, and before matter and form existed.

CH'I – To the Taoist Chinese, the cosmic energy that animates the human body as well as the landscape. Similar to the Hindu or Buddhist term kundalini.

COSMIC SERPENT (snake, dragon) – A symbol of sexual and spiritual energy, often associated with early Earth Mother or goddess cults.

CREATION MYTHS – Stories of early cultures that described the origin of the world, often through the metaphor of gods and goddesses courting and mating.

CREATRIX – Goddess of creativity and matrix of all created in the physical world.

DHARMA – The 'truth' of life and the resultant path one follows.

EROS PRINCIPLE – The mechanism of sexual attraction that animates all nature and particularly love between women and men.

ESOTERIC KNOWLEDGE – Hidden wisdom carried by religious teachings, and particularly by initiates.

EVE – The first woman, companion of Adam, symbolic of the feminine principle.

FEMININE PRINCIPLE – Qualities that are carried by women, but also by men as their shadow, considered to be the unconscious, subjectivity and timelessness, qualities often associated with the right side of the brain.

FENG SHUI – The Chinese art and science of siting buildings in the landscape and also the process of aligning with life energies.

GAIA HYPOTHESIS – Theory of James Lovelock stating that earth is a sentient organism, of which all life is a part.

GNOSTICISM – 'Gnosis' is direct knowing. Many early Christians who held unorthodox ideas about sexuality and reincarnation were considered heretics or gnostics.

GOLDEN FLOWER – A Chinese meditation practice, the purpose of which is to integrate the psyche.

GREAT GODDESS – The primary creative deity governing the fruits of earth, symbolized as the eternal feminine and portrayed as a pregnant Earth Mother.

HORUS – Egyptian god of the sun, who fought a duel with Set to avenge the killing of Osiris. Horus ruled Egypt as the first pharaoh and became the eternal eye of Ra.

I CHING – The famous Chinese 'Book of Changes' describes the interactions of the ch'i energy force, the dancing energies of Yin and Yang.

ISIS – Egyptian goddess of harvest, sister and consort of Osiris.

KABBALA – The Hebrew mystical alphabet correlated letters with numbers, and this magical Judaic tradition described a cosmology of the soul.

KALI – The Hindu and Buddhist great goddess of conception, time and death, often portrayed as a hideous and terrifying dark demon of destruction.

KAMA – Hindu god of love, son of Lakshmi.

KARMA – The system of checks and balances of action and reaction in the world.

KUNDALINI – The spiritual and sexual life force, often seen as female, and symbolized by the coiled serpent or dragon asleep at the base of the spine.

LAKSHMI – The Hindu goddess of good luck. Her name also means lotus or yoni, and she is the mother of Kama, the god of love.

LEY LINES – Energy lines that criss-cross the earth's surface. They carry earth energy from place to place and are the earth equivalent to the Chinese meridians (q.v.).

LOTUS – The flower that symbolizes creation and unfolding, as well as being the earth itself. It also means original spiritual state enclosed with the heart.

LIBIDO – Life energy, correlated with the kundalini force of the Hindus.

MAITHUNA – Ritual sexual union, often accompanied by mantra, yantra and mudras.

MALE PRINCIPLE – Qualities that are carried by men, but also by women, considered as being consciousness, objectivity and linearity, qualities often associated with the left side of the brain.

MANDALA – A consecrated area, usually a circular diagram or geometrical projection of the world reduced to an essential pattern used for meditation, ritual or liturgy.

MANTRA – A sacred sound or series of sounds, used to induce meditation or accumulate cosmic energies.

MĀYĀ – The illusion that constitutes the outer appearance of the world, which hides the true nature of the soul (ātman).

MERIDIANS – Subtle energy channels throughout the body along which sexual and psychic energy passes; the foundation of chinese medicine and sexual yoga.

MUDRA – Ritual hand or foot gestures used in yoga and especially in ritual sexual union.

MYSTERIES (Egyptian, Hermopolitan, Eleusinian) – Religious rituals that express the hidden meaning of life and death.

NUT – Egyptian sky goddess.

ORGONE ENERGY – Life energy transmitted by the sun to all living beings, according to the psychologist Wilhelm Reich, who coined the term.

OSIRIS – Son of the Egyptian sky goddess Nut and elder brother to Isis, Set, Nephthys and Anubis, he was the first king of Egypt. His consort was his sister Isis. He became King of the Dead and overseer of the rituals of the dying.

PISTIS – The Gnostic principle of faith symbolized as being feminine.

POLARITY – The interplay of opposites which attract and repel each other. Also the energetic interaction between sexes.

PRĀNA – Hindu and Buddhist term for breath, which means 'vital force'.

Glossary

RA (RE) – The sun and creator god of Egypt, symbolizing the source of all life as internal fire.

REBIRTH/REINCARNATION – The principle of the soul passing at death to another body and carrying traces of past lives into new life according to the principle of karma.

SERPENT – A symbol of sexual, spiritual energy or the kundalini force. It corresponds to Carl Jung's concept of the libido, but is also an ancient symbol of the great goddess or Earth Mother.

SHAKTI – The divine motive force of the universe and consort of Shiva.

SHIVA – The personification of pure consciousness in the universe, supreme cognition and the vehicle of god.

SOPHIA (WISDOM) - The gnostic principle of wisdom symbolized as being feminine.

TAO TE CHING – Chinese philosophy of Lao Tsu expressed as the harmony and flow of life energy.

TAOISM – The teaching of the 'way', based upon the source of all things, and containing an esoteric, magical alchemy teaching.

TANTRISM – A Hindu and Buddhist philosophy and meditation system, often associated with sexual magic and alchemy.

THEOSOPHICAL SOCIETY – Organization founded by Madame Blavatsky in 1875 to explore and pass on an integration of eastern wisdom and western mystery teachings.

TREE OF LIFE – Symbolizes growth, generation from the seed, emergence from the earth and underworld, an axis linking different worlds, and the entanglement of male and female principles in sexuality. Also known as the Tree of Knowledge.

URAEUS HEADDRESS – Egyptian cobra symbolic of duality and sexual energy.

VISHNU – Hindu creator and sustaining god who participates in a continual and repeating cosmic myth. Upon death he will take a new body and create a new world.

WHEEL OF SAMSARA - The world as an eternal round of conception, birth, old age and death, followed by rebirth in another body. Enlightenment is the only escape.

WORLD EGG – Seed of generation, cosmic symbol of the layers of the heavens above and hells below, and an image of immortality in many early cultures.

YANTRA – A mandala diagram usually simpler in form, which symbolizes the essential energies in the world and spiritual processes, used for ritual or meditative purposes.

YIN/YANG – Passive and active energies that are never separated, and which come together in everything manifest in the world, according to Chinese Taoist philosophy.

YUGA – A Hindu designation of world ages that vary in length from 360,000 to 1,400,000 earth years.

YOGA – Spiritual practice generating concentration and discipline, both mentally and physically.

Index